Praise for

"Readers will be fascinated as the twins recount and reflect on the stresses and daily terrors of becoming refugees. . . . A haunting reminder of how precious democracy is."
—*Kirkus Reviews*

"The Zalli twins powerfully detail the emotional tides and revelations . . . in the Albanian experience and stories of refugee survival, prejudice, and integration."
—*Midwest Book Review*

"An inspirational, evocative book. . . . Now both leading world scientists, Argita and Detina have created a remarkable work, one that will linger long after the reading is done."
—Paul Rosenberg, award-winning leadership coach,
speaker, and strategist

"An engaging, thoughtful book based on a real-life story. . . . Perhaps [it] will change your world outlook, make you consider helping refugee children, or ponder what you can do to ensure that such tragedies never happen again."
—Julia Brodsky, STEM education researcher
and former NASA astronaut instructor

"The story of the Zalli family is the most inspirational example I've ever seen of how the power of love and the positive attitude it creates can transform misfortune into success."
—J. D. Freedman, writer and filmmaker

Good Morning, Hope

A True Story of Refugee Twin Sisters
and Their Triumph over War,
Poverty, and Heartbreak

Argita and Detina Zalli

SANDRA JONAS
PUBLISHING

Sandra Jonas Publishing
PO Box 20892
Boulder, CO 80308
sandrajonaspublishing.com

Printed in the United States of America
28 27 26 25 24 23   2 3 4 5 6 7 8

Cover and book design: Sandra Jonas
Author photograph: Fadil Berisha

Publisher's Cataloging-in-Publication Data

Names: Zalli, Argita, author. | Zalli, Detina, author.
Title: Good Morning, Hope: A True Story of Refugee Twin Sisters and Their
    Triumph over War, Poverty, and Heartbreak / Argita and Detina Zalli.
Description: Boulder, CO : Sandra Jonas Publishing, 2023.
Identifiers: LCCN 2022949610 | ISBN 9781954861053 (hardcover)
    9781954861060 (paperback)
Subjects: LCSH: Zalli, Argita. | Zalli, Detina. | Women refugees –
    Biography. | Albanians – England – Biography. | Twins – Biography.
    | Women scientists – Biography. | Resilience. | LCGFT:
    Autobiographies. | BISAC: BIOGRAPHY & AUTOBIOGRAPHY /
    Personal Memoirs.
Classification: LCC HV640 Z35 | DDC 362.870922
LC record available at http://lccn.loc.gov/2022949610

All the family photographs are from the authors' private collection.

To our mom and dad,
who sacrificed everything to give us a brighter future.
We will never be able to thank you enough.

"Hope" Is the Thing with Feathers
BY EMILY DICKINSON

"Hope" is the thing with feathers —
That perches in the soul —
And sings the tune without the words —
And never stops — at all —

And sweetest — in the Gale — is heard —
And sore must be the storm —
That could abash the little Bird
That kept so many warm —

I've heard it in the chillest land —
And on the strangest Sea —
Yet, never, in Extremity,
It asked a crumb — of Me.

Contents

Authors' Note

We have done our best to present our story as accurately as possible. Our parents, other family members, and friends helped verify our memories. The names of some individuals and locations have been changed to protect privacy.

PART ONE

Albania

CHAPTER 1

Chaos

Deti

March 1, 1997

The moment it all began, my sister and I were playing kickball in the courtyard of our apartment building. Our friends had just gone inside for lunch. Their dolls lay scattered on the patches of grass, waiting for everyone to return. Mom would call us in soon.

The score was eight to three, and I was in the lead, as usual. Smiling, I pointed at Gita and then took aim and kicked the ball hard and high, the dirt rising up in a cloud. As planned, it soared over her head and I scored another point. Only one more and I would win. That was the rule—whoever made it to ten first was the champion.

She scurried after the ball and got ready to kick it back. "You haven't won yet," she called out.

"But I will!" I threw off my jacket, suddenly warm as the sun broke through the clouds. Bending my knees, I bounced from one foot to the other, waiting. She was taking forever. "C'mon, Gita."

"Okay, okay."

It was no secret that Gita hated kickball. My twin sister and I were identical in so many ways, but not when it came to sports. She played to make me happy, and I loved her for it.

To keep her in the game, I always let her score a couple of points. Otherwise, who would play with me? For sure, none of the other girls. And Gita said she had heard that the boys wouldn't invite me back for another soccer game because I'd scored too many goals. They were embarrassed to lose to a girl. Well, they could pick up all my tricks by watching the Italian and Brazilian players on TV like I did. Silly boys.

Gita brought her foot back, about to kick, when a strange cracking sound pierced the air. "What was that?" She turned around and looked behind her.

"It's nothing. Kick the ball!"

Then it happened again. And again.

The next time, the sound whooshed right by my ear, and a chill rushed down my spine. "Someone's shooting at us!"

The bullets came fast now, ricocheting off the old brick walls and windows. Glass shattered. I froze.

"Run, Deti!" Gita yelled.

She flew past me and glanced over her shoulder to make sure I was following her. "Hurry!"

Another spray of bullets. And then another. Across the way, kids and grown-ups ran in all directions, screaming.

"The ball!" I yelled to her.

"Leave it!"

"I can't." It was only a few meters away. I had to save it. How would we ever get a new one? Dropping to the ground, I crawled on my belly.

"Get inside!" Mom yelled from the upstairs window.

Gita crouched down and grabbed my shirt. "We have to go NOW!"

"Don't—I'm coming!"

I tried to wrestle away, but she yanked with all the strength of her eleven years and more. As I stretched out my arm and reached for the ball, one of the bullets hit it. Air escaped through a gaping hole in its beautiful shiny body, and it spun across the courtyard, landing in a heap. My stomach heaved as if someone had punched me.

The gunfire was coming from every direction. We'd never make it inside. Gita and I scrambled to the nearest bush and ducked behind it. The leaves and branches scraped our faces and tore at our clothes.

Everything was getting louder. The bullets popping and cracking, the glass shattering, the screaming. So much screaming.

"Deti! Gita!" Dad yelled through the noise.

He was so close yet separated by such a dangerous little strip. I peered over the bush to look at him.

Gita tugged on my wrist. "Keep your head *down!*"

My sister, my protector. Always. I clung to her. My teeth began to chatter, and I couldn't make them stop.

"Mom? Dad?" We both yelled out at the same time.

"Don't move!" Dad yelled back. "Don't move!"

Minutes passed, each one lasting forever. Gita and I hugged and cried, our faces pressed together, our bodies shaking.

A man's gruff voice made us jump. "You're dead!" he yelled. Then came the sharp rattle of his gun, and rounds and rounds of bullets whistled past us.

I gasped, almost crying out. Gita put her finger to my lips. "Shhh," she mouthed, her dark eyes wide with fear, no doubt mirroring my own.

His shadow fell over us. He wore a black coat, and a long ponytail ran down the middle of his back. Only a couple of steps away. He carried an AK-47.

My teeth chattered even harder. Gita clamped her hand over my mouth. I tasted dirt and sweat.

"You're dead!" he yelled again, and let loose with more gunfire.

We waited, holding our breath. My legs and back ached fiercely. *Dear God, please help us.*

After what seemed like hours, but was probably just seconds, the man ran off, and the shooting finally stopped. Everything went still. Gita took her hand from my mouth.

"Let's go," I whispered, starting to get to my feet.

"No, Deti, a little longer, to make sure."

"Stay there!" Dad yelled out to us.

More waiting. And then shoes crunched over the broken glass, and Dad knelt down to wrap his arms around us. "It's all right. I'm here. You're safe."

I leaned into him with relief, my body still shaking. When he lifted us up, I saw the blood on his shirt sleeve. "Dad, you're bleeding!"

"It's nothing. Just a scratch from the broken window."

Just a scratch? The blood was pouring out of his arm.

Mom rushed to us and buried her face in our shoulders. "Thank God, you're okay."

"Dad's hurt," I told her. "He's bleeding." I pushed away and took off running.

"Where are you going, Deti? Wait!" Gita called out.

Without answering, I bounded up to our apartment as fast as I could. The staircase was tight and dark, many of the steps chipped or broken. My knee bumped into a step past the second floor. Number 45. Gita and I had numbered all the steps to our fourth-floor apartment, 128 altogether. We raced each other up and down all the time. I always won, and that day, I knew I'd break my one-minute record.

My knee throbbed, but I ignored the pain. When I reached the fourth floor, I threw open our door and darted into the bathroom for a towel. Where had Mom put the raki? We helped Grandpa Llazi make the potent drink from the grapes after they had been pressed for wine. The high alcoholic content also made it an excellent antiseptic.

I found the bottle inside the kitchen cupboard and ran back down the stairs. At the third floor, Gita, Mom, and Dad were there to meet me. I wanted to stop the bleeding and medicate the cut on Dad's arm right away.

"No, Deti, not here. Let's get inside first."

As we climbed the stairs, a terrified silence filled the air. Hearing our footsteps, our neighbors opened their door.

"Jesus, what happened?" Mr. Braka hurried over to Dad and examined his arm.

I never took my eyes off Dad. He smiled because he couldn't cry, but his face was pale.

"You're lucky, Gimi," Mr. Braka said. "It isn't a deep cut. You won't need any stitches. Come in. I'll clean that up for you and bandage it."

Inside their apartment, Mr. Braka made Dad sit on a chair in the kitchen to check his arm more carefully. "I used to do this all the time in the army." He liked to tell everyone his war stories. Gita and I called him "Sir Captain."

Mr. Braka took the bottle of raki, and I eyed him anxiously. "Are you sure you can do this? Please don't hurt him."

He smiled and patted my arm. "He won't even feel it."

Mr. Braka elevated Dad's arm and examined the wound. Using tweezers, he removed a few pieces of glass still stuck in the cut and then took a clean rag and applied firm pressure on the wound. Once the bleeding stopped, he used a new rag soaked with raki and firmly tied it in place.

Slowly, the color returned to Dad's face, and I started to breathe easier. Gita too. I squeezed her hand and she squeezed mine back. Miracle of all miracles, none of us had gotten seriously hurt. Dad was going to be okay. We went into the living room, and Mrs. Braka gave us candies to take our minds off everything. The grown-ups talked in hushed tones, their faces creased with worry.

It was dark when we finally went to our apartment. Broken glass was scattered all over the living room floor.

"Girls, stay back." Dad waved us out of the room.

We watched from the doorway as they cleaned up the mess. Gita and I looked at each other and back at Mom and Dad. What had happened today? What was the shooting all about? Had anyone died? Were the gunmen coming back?

So many questions.

We didn't know it yet, but our beloved Albania was unraveling. And soon it would collapse, along with everything we held dear.

CHAPTER 2

Don't Shoot Us

Gita

March 14, 1997

Our mother always wanted us to be doctors. Growing up poor, one of ten children, she dreamed of a better life for her daughters that would give them everything she never had.

Night after night, she read to us, quizzing us, coaching us, hugging us, her green eyes sparkling with excitement as she planned our grand future. Before we even started school, she gave us Italian lessons, and then she and Dad scrimped and saved to hire tutors to teach us English.

Someday, Deti and I would move to the United States, Mom said, and make our mark in medicine.

We shared her dream—there was no job more important than being a doctor. On our third birthday, our grandfather gave us a doctor's play kit, and we practiced on each other and on our friends, taking the stethoscope with us everywhere we went. We wanted to be the best.

But now that dream seemed impossible.

In the days following the shooting in the courtyard, armed gangs started appearing all around us. No matter how hard we tried to ignore them by staying busy and studying for long hours, we could feel the tension rising. We weren't safe anymore.

On Friday afternoon, Deti and I were in math class with Mrs. Ramina. She was strict. She wanted us to excel, so there was no room for error. If you weren't prepared and didn't give the right answers to her questions, she didn't hesitate to slap you or ridicule you in front of the others.

Fridays were always quiz days, and even though they scared me, they helped me forget the harsh reality of our country. The walls of the school seem to hold back the world—a temporary escape from the sudden sprays of gunfire or the deafening thumps of bombs and grenades. Each Friday, as soon as all thirty students filed into the classroom, Mrs. Ramina passed out the weekly quiz, and without a word, everybody set to work.

Within seconds, silence filled the air, creating an atmosphere of total tranquility. The only sound I heard was the scraping of our pencils or an occasional grunt and sigh from one of the students struggling with a problem. Deti sat next to me and wrote quickly. She knew the answers to all the questions—as usual. Out of the corner of my eye, I could see we had only fifteen minutes left. Deti put down her pen. She was finished.

I was still working on the last problem. A hard one. Deti glanced at me. "I'll tell you the answer," she said with her eyes.

"No," I whispered. "Too risky."

Ignoring me, Deti quickly wrote out the answer on a tiny piece of paper, cupped it into the palm of her hand, and turned it toward me. I was too afraid to look at it. Cheating would mean punishment for both of us.

"Just take it," she whispered. "You don't have time."

Deti would hate it if she got an A and I didn't. Everything in me was part of her too. It took two As for us to succeed. As identical twins, we needed to do everything together. Wherever Deti went, I wasn't far behind. Wherever I went, she wasn't far behind.

I scanned the room. What should I do? Mrs. Ramina was staring out the window.

Now, I told myself. The perfect time to—

Suddenly, Mrs. Ramina turned and rushed to the middle of the room. "Get under your desks!" she shouted.

I jumped in surprise and dropped my pencil. Thirty heads bobbed up in unison from their tests as Mrs. Ramina locked the door and barricaded it with her giant wooden desk. I grabbed Deti's arm and pulled her to the floor. Frantic, Mrs. Ramina went from one window to the next, closing and locking them. There was nothing but tiny locks to hold them closed.

From outside, tires crunching over gravel, brakes squealing, doors slamming, and then silence, but not for long. Young male voices started yelling and swearing furiously.

Like in the courtyard, bullets cracked in the air and burst mercilessly through the windows. Did anyone get hurt? Where did the bullets land?

More cracking, more broken glass littering the floor. These monsters were everywhere. Mrs. Ramina had us crawl as far away from the windows as possible so we wouldn't get hurt. She huddled with us under the desks.

Silence again. We waited, our ears straining to hear the next burst, but then came a click followed by a violent bang. Click, bang, slam—it seemed to be traveling down the hallway.

"They're inside the school!" Mrs. Ramina whispered.

Heavy boots clomping. A flurry of angry voices. So young. They had to be gang boys. My blood ran cold.

Deti and I scrunched together, trying to be smaller, trying to get closer. I could feel her heart beating, just like my own. Two hearts, one body.

My face was wet. Was I crying or were they Deti's tears? It made no difference. Mine were hers. Under the desks, the rows of faces looked the same. Pale, silent, all eyes dark with terror, holding unshed tears, lips mouthing prayers.

Volleys of bullets echoed loudly in the hallway. What if the boys came into our classroom?

Mrs. Ramina shouted, "Heads down! Stay where you are! Don't be afraid!"

Don't be afraid? How could she say that? We could hear other kids screaming and crying. My teeth were clenched so hard my jaw and face hurt. Tears dripped off my chin. Luckily Mrs. Ramina had locked the door, and so far, no one had shot out the locks and tried to enter.

Finally, the sound of sirens. The police! For a moment the tightness in my chest relaxed, but then I realized the armed gang was still inside the building. More shouting and scuffling in the halls.

Would the police have to storm our school and get into a shoot-out with the boys? And what if we were caught in their crossfire? Even if we weren't, if the boys won the fight, they would break into our classroom, line us up, and shoot us, one by one.

How much would it hurt? How long would the pain last?

Suddenly, someone rapped on the door, and Mrs. Ramina scrambled to her feet. "Who's there?" she asked, her voice trembling. One of the strongest women I knew was scared. And there was nothing she could do to protect us if gunmen were behind the door.

"Police!" came the answer.

Mrs. Ramina removed the barricade, and several officers strode into the room. "You're safe now," they said, before conducting a quick sweep of the room and leaving just as quickly as they had arrived. Methodically, the officers moved through the other classrooms and then went outside to secure the building.

Slowly, still shaking, Deti and I crawled out from under our desks, our clothes rumpled, our eyes and faces stained with tears. A wave of relief washed over me. I felt both elated and crushed, strangely empty, like I'd been squeezed through a juicer.

"We made it!" Mrs. Ramina called out, her voice sounding stronger. "It's over."

I was still holding Deti's hand. I'd been holding it for so long and so tightly that I didn't feel my fingers. The gangsters might have been gone, but I was still terrified.

"Everything is going to be all right," Mrs. Ramina kept saying. She wiped our friend Vera's eyes as she held on to her tightly. Then Mrs. Ramina made her way to the rest of the class, hugging each child, wiping away the tears, and calming down the ones who couldn't stop shaking. She was no longer a dictator to us. Now, she was a second mother, loving and caring.

Before the police left, they returned to our classroom to question Mrs. Ramina one last time. I heard them telling her that the teachers across the hall had seen three young boys. They weren't known gangsters, the police said, and if they had intended to kill anybody, they would have already done it.

The worst part was that they had been students of the school. They had all dropped out at age fourteen. Army depots were now run by teenagers who had no qualms about arming other teenagers or children with guns. Child soldiers were becoming common. They couldn't read, write, or spell, but they could take lives at the pull of a trigger.

They didn't need to waste their time getting an education, listening to rules, and being punished. They could make their own rules now. They had their guns, and we could keep our books.

The policemen were kind and reassuring, but their words weren't enough to protect us. After today and the experience in the courtyard, it was the policemen's guns and whips I wanted to see next to me.

The boys might come back. Who could assure us that they wouldn't kill someone the next time?

By now, guns and rioting were everywhere in Albania. The government issued an order to close the schools for the next several weeks. The ones that remained open weren't safe. We spent four long months cooped up inside the house, reading, studying, and watching TV.

We saw reports on the terrible killings, of civilians and deputies fighting one another all over the country. Many people said that officials had been running Ponzi schemes, stealing from ordinary citizens like Mom and Dad, and the government collapsed. The news showed thousands of armed protesters demanding their money back. Day after day, the demonstrations continued, even in our small town of Patos.

Foreign countries started to evacuate their citizens. Who could blame them? Thousands of Albanians had lost not only their savings, but also their jobs, and poverty was getting worse. People tried to take revenge by burning the customs posts and tax offices.

A large part of the country was no longer under the government's control. The neighbors said there was no more law in Albania, and the gangs, many of them tied to the Mafia, had taken over. Until that fateful day when the young boys stormed the school with their guns, I hadn't understood, but I did now.

We prayed for our country.

We prayed for ourselves.

And we asked God to help us get out of Albania alive.

CHAPTER 3

Nowhere Safe

Deti

June 4, 1997

Silence filled the streets. Day after day, we stayed locked inside our apartment, shrouded in fear so real it seemed to live in the shadows, like another member of our family.

"When will it be safe to play outside again?" We kept asking.

As the days became weeks, the wall of fear grew taller and larger. At night when the shadows descended, every sound outside, every voice, set us on edge.

After a while, though, some of the people in the city started to venture out of their homes, but Mom and Dad still held us back. They wanted to be sure.

In June, the schools reopened for summer classes, and many of our friends were allowed outside. I talked to them from our balcony. They even traveled by bus with their parents to Vlorë Beach, forty-five kilometers from Patos.

"Mom and Dad, please, can't we go to the beach like everyone else?" I asked.

It had been two years since we had all gone together. That summer, Dad kept saying he would take us, but he had to work every weekend. Finally, he told us, "I promise we'll go this Sunday."

But when Sunday arrived, it was chilly and rainy. We went to the beach anyway and huddled under an umbrella on the sand. "A promise is a promise," Dad said, his arms around us.

Now, two summers later, Gita joined in to plead with him and Mom. "Things have been calmer lately. We can't stay inside forever. We've been prisoners for four months."

Mom and Dad exchanged glances. They didn't say no right away, so I took a chance. "Will you please take us to the beach this weekend?" I crossed my fingers.

Dad looked at me first, then at Gita. "Okay, we'll take you to the beach on Saturday. But we must all stay together. Agreed?" He reached out and squeezed Gita's hand.

Her face lit up and she laughed. "Yes!" we both said. "Thank you, thank you, thank you!"

We gave him a big hug and then turned to Mom and hugged her too. She kissed us tenderly on our cheeks, holding both of us close. I couldn't help but see the tears in her eyes. What a horrible four months it had been for all of us.

Gita and I were so excited we could hardly eat supper. But it was only Wednesday. Two more long days, still locked up in our prison.

Finally, Friday evening arrived, and we eagerly climbed into bed. I watched Gita fall asleep, but I had too many thoughts crowding my head. Too many visions of what it would be like to ride on the bus and see the city streets, the beautiful Albanian countryside, our friends— and then the beach. I couldn't wait to squish the sand between my toes and walk along the shore, to feel the warm ocean water lapping my feet.

The hands on the clock moved painfully slowly. I might have dozed off a few times, but not for long. How could Gita just lie there so peacefully, so totally asleep, as if tomorrow were like any other day?

I counted down the hours from midnight. One o'clock . . . two . . . two-thirty . . . four. I couldn't stand it anymore. Leaning over and giving my sister a shake, I whispered in her ear, "Gita, wake up! It's almost time to go."

Gita rolled over and eyed me sleepily. "What?" she murmured. "What time is it?" She lifted her head and twisted her neck to look at the clock. "Deti, it's only four in the morning. Are you crazy?"

"Will you come with me to wake up Mom and Dad?"

"In the middle of the night? No way." Gita pulled the covers over her head and rolled over. "Go back to sleep."

"I can't."

"It's too early," she grumbled, and instantly fell back asleep.

I was so wide awake I couldn't possibly crawl under the covers again. There was nothing wrong with waking up Mom and Dad, but I didn't want to do it by myself. I needed Gita with me.

Then I knew exactly what to do.

Gita loved chocolate, especially the small squares of Belgian milk chocolate. She always hid her stash, afraid I'd steal it. But she didn't know that one day when I was looking for some cheese in the fridge, I found her precious chocolate way in the back on the lower shelf, carefully wrapped in foil.

Feeling wicked, I giggled to myself as I pushed my feet into my slippers and crept out to the kitchen. When I opened the fridge, it let out a soft moan, but the kitchen was too far away for anyone to hear. I reached down behind a tub of butter and pulled out Gita's package of chocolate. Removing four small squares, I put them in a paper napkin and crept back to the bedroom.

Gently I tweaked Gita's ear. She opened one eye and groaned. "Oh no. It's you again."

"Yes, just me." I smiled sweetly. Placing the napkin of chocolate where Gita could see it, I picked up one piece and slowly moved it in the direction of my waiting mouth.

Her eyes flew open, and she shot up in bed. "You, you thief. That's mine!" She snatched the piece away from me and popped it into her mouth.

"A chocolate a day keeps Gita awake." I laughed.

She looked down at the napkin and grinned. "Okay, you win. You can have half." She popped a second piece into her mouth.

"I can hear sounds coming from Mom and Dad's bedroom. I think they're up."

"I doubt it."

But she realized I wouldn't take no for an answer. She followed me into the hallway and stood behind me as I knocked on Mom and Dad's door. Gita was right. After a few minutes, we heard Mom's sleepy voice. "It's too early. Go back to bed. Now!"

Sheepishly we returned to our bedroom. I crawled into Gita's bed, and she held me close until I finally fell asleep.

The bus to Vlorë Beach was filled with many of our friends and their parents. We sang and chattered like magpies. It was so long since we'd seen one another.

Who cared if the outing was for just one day? We were free.

It was such a perfect day to be at the beach. Maybe what made it so perfect was our appreciation and gratitude for the freedom that before now we took for granted. As a gentle breeze riffled the warm, clean waters of the Adriatic Sea and the white sand sparkled in the dazzling summer sun, we laughed and played as never before.

"Who wants ice cream?" Mom called to us after a while. At once we ran back to where we put our blankets and beach bags. Dad scrambled to his feet and took our hands, leading us over the boardwalk to the row of concessions.

There were too many flavors to choose from, so Dad let us have double-dip cones. He also treated us to some chocolate, as we knew he would. After that, we headed back to the beach and had fun playing ball with him, laughing and scrambling in the sand until it was time to cool off in the water again.

"Who wants to learn how to swim?" he asked.

"Me!" we both shouted.

Dad started with teaching us how to float. He showed us how to arch our backs, lift our legs, and let go. As he guided me, his hands underneath me, I understood perfectly, or rather my body understood perfectly, how to let myself gently float. It worked. I tilted upward again, laughing.

Then it was Gita's turn. Oh, how she struggled with letting go.

"I'm right here to catch you," Dad said.

But something inside wouldn't let Gita lift her feet. It was a matter of trust. She continued to resist, unable to take a leap of faith for something as natural and harmless as learning to float in the sea.

At three o'clock, it was time to dust off the sand, pack up our things, and head home. We joined our friends and piled into the bus, sunburned, sandy, tired, and oh so happy and grateful for the day.

We settled into our seats, listening to the steady grinding of the tires and the hum of the motor as the bus sped over the countryside. Lulled by the sounds of the happy chattering and the steady sounds of the bus, Gita and I closed our eyes and drifted off peacefully.

Suddenly through the deep layers of contentment, someone shouted, "No!"

It was the driver.

"No!" he shouted again.

I bolted upright. "What's wrong?" I shook Gita's hand. She opened her eyes and stared at me, angry at the rude awakening.

The bus lurched to a stop. Propping myself up on my knees, I looked out the window. Three men stood in front of the bus, their faces covered in black ski masks. They were tall with athletic builds. On their shoulders were weapons. AK-47s.

Icy terror crawled through me. More gangsters. They pounded on the door, forcing the driver to open it. My heart raced wildly as my mind struggled to register what was happening. Not again!

"Gita, it's them," I whispered.

"Who?" she whispered back.

She stiffened. She knew. She saw. Both of us stared at the three men entering the bus. We stared at their weapons.

The men strode up the aisle, looking at each of us as they passed. All we could see were their eyes, one pair of blue eyes and two pairs of black eyes. All three pairs were cold and cruel.

Dad and Mom leaned over and whispered to us, "Don't worry, everything will be okay."

"How do you know that?" I choked back tears.

The men walked back to the front of the bus. One of them said in a harsh, demanding voice, "All we want is your money and anything else that's valuable. We don't want to hurt you. If you are carrying gold, silver, or any kind of jewelry, hand it over. The sooner you give it to us, the sooner we'll be gone."

A collective sad sigh passed through the bus as everyone shifted in their seats and reached into their pockets to empty them. The women unfastened the chains around their necks and slid their bracelets and rings from their wrists and fingers. The men, including my dad, opened up their wallets. All the men did this except one, an older guy with gray hair and black eyes who sat opposite us. He bent over to get his bag from under the seat. While reaching for it, he deftly placed 10,000 lek inside his left sock.

What was he doing? If I could see him, so could the gangsters. They said that nothing would happen to us if we gave them all our money. What would they do when they discovered what he was hiding?

I stared at the hooded monsters as they passed through the bus, collecting everyone's money and valuables. When they reached the gray-haired man, he handed them over nothing but his empty wallet.

"Where's your money?" they shouted.

"I don't have any," the man said calmly.

"Yeah, we'll see about that. If you're lying, you'll be saying goodbye to this world today." The gangsters checked his jeans and top pockets. Finding nothing in them, they asked him to take off his shoes.

The man followed their orders without arguing. The gangsters examined the shoes thoroughly and found nothing again.

"Take off your socks!"

My heart almost stopped. The gangsters would see that he was trying to hide his money. It would make them angry. He was about to be shot in front of our very eyes.

The man slowly, carefully, rolled his right sock down his foot and then the left one. While he seemed unfazed, his hands trembled after he removed both socks.

The tension was too much for me. I closed my eyes, but my ears strained, ready to hear the terrifying sound of the AK-47.

Long seconds passed. When would it happen? Why was no one speaking? Were they getting ready to shoot him?

"It's your lucky day," one of the gangsters said.

I opened my eyes, and the three men continued to pass through the bus, collecting money and valuables. It was a miracle. How did the man get out of that alive?

When the gangsters reached us, Dad gave them all his money and Mom gave them a couple of rings, including her precious engagement ring. Seeing the sadness on her face, I wanted to shout at them, "You are evil men. You have no soul!"

I knew better. We weren't out of danger yet. If I dared to speak out, one of the men could instantly whip around and point his gun at me or at my sister and my parents. I sat as still as I could, not moving a muscle until the thieves, finally satisfied with their loot, stomped off the bus.

Immediately, the bus door closed, and wordlessly, the driver turned the key in the ignition. He drove fast, never taking his foot off the gas pedal.

I glanced over at Mom. She slid her fingers under the edge of her elastic sleeve and pulled out her wedding band. How had she managed that? It was so clever, so brave—and so risky. But that ring was very special to her.

No one in the bus spoke. Shock has no words. The thieves hadn't just robbed us. They also stole the sense of contentment and security that had wrapped everyone a few minutes earlier. The happy chatter was gone. The bus droned on in silence, the steady hum of the motor no longer comforting.

CHAPTER 4

Holdup

Deti

September 25, 1997

Dad worked in the offices of Albpetrol, a state-owned oil company. Over the last few chaotic months, like many other public and private institutions, most of the offices of Albpetrol had been broken into and vandalized, some of them even burned.

We pleaded with Dad not to go to work anymore. It was too dangerous. He'd been lucky so far. When the gangsters ransacked the offices of Albpetrol, he hadn't been there. Dad didn't seem to realize how fortunate he had been, making me more afraid for him.

He said that Albpetrol and other large businesses were trying to repair the damage as quickly as possible and restore order. By the end of September, our lives seemed to be calmer, but we weren't the ones who had to go work so far away from home. We were only allowed to play in the courtyard, a sheltered area.

Nevertheless, the board members of Albpetrol decided that in addition to hiring security guards to patrol the buildings and grounds, they would also install a staff representative to stay on duty at all times. Each staff member was assigned a shift.

When Dad's turn came, he was expected to be on duty from midnight until six the next evening—eighteen long hours. At our usual bedtime, he would come in and kiss us good night. He always wore a gray suit and crisp white shirt, a handkerchief in his breast pocket. Mom made sure his clothes were immaculate and pressed.

His dark hair was starting to thin, but he was still the most handsome man to us.

He would wish us sweet dreams—though there was little sweetness in our dreams then. Our dreams had become filled with fears. Every time Dad left for his shift, Gita and I barely slept, worrying if he would be all right.

One night, just before he left, I heard Mom begging him, "Please, Gimi, promise me if you run into any problems, you'll call Berti and Nori."

We didn't have a phone, so we had to rely on the neighbors and relatives for any type of immediate contact when any of us was away from home. Our uncles, Berti and Nori, had a reputation in Patos for being strong, fearless men. Maybe they could keep Dad safe.

"Yes, yes, of course," Dad said softly to Mom. "But I'm sure everything will be fine."

The next day, he came home early from his shift looking tired and depleted, more so than normal. As we set the table for dinner, he paid close attention to all of us. He ate very little, his eyes glistening with tears, and then excused himself from the table, saying he was tired and wanted to go to bed.

In the morning, for the first time, he didn't go to work. He rested, ate, and watched TV with us all day. Our prayers had been answered, yet we noticed a change in him. He still radiated strength, but he was extra quiet, subdued.

What had happened?

Gita and I asked Mom, but she didn't know. Dad had never missed a day of work, and when she asked him about it, he shook his head and didn't answer. She didn't push him. All that mattered was that he was alive, Mom said. He would tell us when he was ready.

It took Dad seven years to talk about that night.

He had been in his office on the second floor when he received a call a couple of hours into his shift. Jak, a representative of Marinez, a partner company of Albpetrol, told Dad about a theft at their oil extraction department. He talked fast, his voice strained, making it difficult for Dad to catch everything.

"Slow down, Jak, slow down! I can't understand what—"

Just then a security guard burst into his office. He stood at the door, ashen and trembling.

"Jak, wait a minute, would you?"

The security guard could barely speak. "S-s-sir, th-there are armed m-m-men on the first floor. They st-st-stormed into the building."

Dad told Jak to send help and he'd call him back. Hanging up the phone, Dad turned to the man. "Where are the other guards?"

"H-h-hiding. On the third floor."

"*Hiding?*"

He nodded.

"Outrageous!" Cowards. All of them.

That meant Dad was the only one in charge—and he had no gun or any kind of protection. What could he do? His anger started slipping into panic. No, he had to stay calm, focused. He had to think clearly.

The guard slumped against the door, looking like he was about to pass out. Dad led him to a chair. The man would be no help.

Dad took a deep breath. He would go downstairs and talk to them, find out what they wanted. From the head of the stairs, he could see down into the lobby. There were at least five armed men dressed in shades of black and gray. Harsh voices, all of them snarling among themselves, like a pack of wolves on the hunt.

Now Dad understood why the guards were hiding. He almost ran back into his office and locked the door. But he realized they would soon start searching the other floors and he didn't want to be cornered like prey.

He would have to make the first move. Bracing himself, he called down in a loud voice, "My name is Gimi. I am an employee here and I don't have a weapon. I want to talk with you."

Startled, the men swung their weapons in his direction. One of them said, "Come down with your hands up."

Dad raised his hands and walked slowly down the stairs. When he stepped into the lobby, he came face to face with two greasy-looking characters pointing AK-47s at his head. Behind them were three more men, holding an assortment of knives and pistols.

Terrified, Dad did his best to swallow his fear.

"Hello." He was surprised he could speak and that he sounded so casual. Cautiously he started to lower his hands. This sent the whole group into an angry frenzy. All of them yelled "Hands up!" and pointed their guns at him. His arms shot back into the air, his heart thumping wildly.

A rough-looking guy with broad shoulders and thick arms stepped closer. "Who the hell do you think you are?" he growled. He must have been the boss. "How many others are upstairs? Don't lie to us or we'll blow your head off!"

"I'm in charge here. There are five of us. The people upstairs won't come down unless I tell them to."

As the men looked at one another, trying to figure out what to do, Dad studied their faces to memorize them. When he got to the fourth guy, he couldn't believe what he was seeing. The man lived in Berti's neighborhood.

Another minute more and he remembered his name. Tori. There was no mistaking him. He looked like a billy goat. A long, thin face, wide-set eyes, a worried expression, and coarse hair. Dad never liked the man. He was weak and not very smart. Seeing him with this gang reinforced his opinion.

"Tori, you know me, don't you?" Dad asked in the same casual voice. Inside he was falling apart.

"Yeah, I know Gimi, boss," Tori said, waving his AK-47 toward Dad's head. "He won't trick us."

Alarmed, Dad moved slightly to the side. Tori was stupid enough to shoot him by accident.

"Okay," the boss said. "You tell your people to come downstairs from wherever they're hiding. No weapons. One by one with their hands up. They have two minutes."

"Can I call them through the intercom?"

The men looked puzzled.

"It will allow me to broadcast the message to everyone. It's located at the receptionist's desk." Dad nodded toward the desk in the lobby.

"Be our guest," the boss said, but he still followed him and kept the pistol aimed at his head.

Dad picked up the intercom phone and spoke into it. "This is Gimi." His voice echoed throughout the quiet building. "Please drop your weapons and come down to the lobby, one by one with your hands up. You have only two minutes. Do exactly what these men tell you to do."

The three guards hiding on the third floor were the first to walk into the lobby without their weapons, as instructed. The guard in Dad's office was next. The armed thugs ushered everyone into an office and locked them inside.

"Okay then," the boss turned to Dad, wagging the pistol in his face.

He looked into the eyes of this dullard. They were all bullies, cowards, but they were cowards with guns. He had to be careful.

"We're going to take the desktop computers from all the offices," the boss said. "And since you know Tori, you'll have to help us."

"Of course, I'll help you." Inside his head, Dad kept repeating, *All business, stay calm, all business . . .*

The boss studied the map of the building in the lobby. "Let's start with the IT office on the second floor. Probably six computers there. Then we can go to the director's office."

Dad walked toward the stairs, and Tori followed him. Dad had to act now. He had to choose his words carefully and be as calm as possible. "Look, man, we know each other, and I want to give you advice for your own good. You can either take it or not, that's your choice. But I suggest you not do this, because you won't win in the end."

"Hey listen, whoever you are," one of the other men said, "nobody asked for your opinion." He seemed younger than the rest. He cocked his AK at Dad, ready to fire.

The boss whipped around and glared at him. "Shut your mouth, Tare." He turned to Dad. "Explain exactly what you meant. Why did you say that we wouldn't win in the end?"

Relying on the group's stupidity, Dad made up something fast. "The desktops of our company are commissioned, and they can only work here." He lowered his voice. "This is confidential, but they don't function anywhere else."

"So? Who gives a shit if they don't function? And who the hell do you think you are, trying to do our business for us?" He coughed and spat on the polished floor. "We sell the damn stuff and the people who buy them, whadda they know?" The other guys laughed at that. "He thinks he's a wise guy, eh?"

"Of course, you can lie to the buyers, but that's only a short-term solution." Dad decided to try another ploy. "Since the computers are commissioned with our company, they'll be able to track you down afterward. And they'll demand their money back."

The group looked skeptical—but worried. Seeing this, Dad continued talking.

"What do you think will happen once your customers find out that the computers don't work?" He lowered his voice, acting again like he was taking the boss into his confidence. "Everyone is armed nowadays—you could be in worse trouble. I hate to say this, but they might harm you or your family. And remember, this situation in Albania will calm down in the future and order will be restored. Then both of us, you and I, will be responsible for this."

"So you're trying to protect yourself? You coward!" the boss shouted, instantly enraged.

"No, I'm not scared," Dad said, even though he was shaking inside. "I'm just trying to be logical and give you sound advice. I know Tori well. He's my brother-in-law's good friend, so I feel obliged to warn you, since I want nothing bad to happen to any of you."

"Boss, maybe he's right," Tori said. "We can get a lot of money today for these computers, but tomorrow we might be in big trouble. These are crappy tools anyway and they aren't worth taking a risk for." He lowered his voice. "Why don't we go for plan B? We can do that other thing in your town. We still have time."

The boss snorted and cracked his knuckles as he paced back and forth across the lobby. "No," he muttered. "We can't destroy plan A altogether. We *need* to take something from the offices."

Dad's mind started racing when he heard him say that. The guy might be dumb but he was headstrong. What could Dad do? How could he get rid of them?"

He looked around frantically, exploring his options—and then got the perfect idea. The leader of the group had a belly, the belly of a drinker. In Dad's office, he had a bottle of whiskey his cousin Sokol had brought for him from Greece only two days before.

If he offered it to the leader, he might see through it, but if Dad did nothing, the guy might kill him. What choice did he have?

"How about trying a bottle of whiskey from Greece?" he asked the boss. "It's in my office. I can bring it down to you."

Say yes, you dumb oaf, please say yes.

Finally, the boss nodded and waved a hand at Tori to go upstairs with him. Dad quickly grabbed the bottle of whiskey sitting on the shelf behind his desk and returned to the lobby, Tori right at his heels.

Dad handed the bottle to the boss, who opened it and took a swig. "Ahh, this is good whiskey." He took another swig. "It's not like the whiskey these Albanian assholes sell."

"Can I try it, boss?" Tori asked eagerly, his gun still pointed at him. "Take it."

Tori passed the bottle to one of the other guys. Soon everyone took a swig and they relaxed. Sitting in a circle, they propped up their guns and drank a second round.

"I can't believe that my plan failed today," the boss said sadly, his broad shoulders slumping. He shook his massive head. "I just don't get it. So far, none of my plans have worked. It's as if someone has cursed us." His eyes were flashing as he barked to the others, "C'mon. Let's get out of here. On the double." The men groaned as they stood and gathered their weapons.

"And, you, listen here," the boss said, jabbing a finger in Dad's chest, "If anyone speaks of what happened here today, just know one thing. I will come after you and blow your head off."

"You have nothing to worry about," Dad said. "I have never heard of you, never seen you."

The men piled into their van, revved up the engine, and drove off, their tires screeching as they sped down the street. Within a minute or two, the roar of their van faded, and Dad returned to his office and called Jak.

That dark night in September left a deep scar on Dad and the staff, including the security guards on duty. And in the end, Dad's efforts to save the company computers were all in vain. A week later, another gang broke into Albpetrol and made off with the equipment. The other offices that hadn't been damaged were burned to the ground.

Albpetrol was shut down for two weeks. Luckily, when it reopened, Dad and the other employees were transferred to a building with better security measures, and they worked from there. Anyone entering the building was checked for weapons and proper identification.

The life we loved was rapidly being destroyed by ordinary citizens. They had evolved into desperadoes who took what they wanted and killed those who opposed them. Every day, highly respected, hard-working people like my father found their lives in jeopardy.

CHAPTER 5

Guns and Grudges

Deti

November 1997

As the end of the year approached, the streets and public places had become dangerous hot spots for crime. Although we had a new government and the rioting had ended, ruthless gangs of armed Albanians were still our enemy. It was like a war zone. For years, Mom and Dad had been talking about leaving the country. Now, it was more important than ever.

When we were small children, Gita and I would stand on the balcony of our apartment after dinner watching the sky as it grew dark. If we made a wish as soon as the first star appeared, it would come true. We wished the same thing every night: to live in the United States.

We wanted to go to McDonald's and Disneyland and carry a Mickey Mouse backpack to school. Patos was small, and there was so little to do. From what we saw on Albanian TV, we would never be bored in America.

All the kids in our town loved Hollywood action movies. Whenever they came on, we stopped playing and went inside to watch. I imitated Sylvester Stallone's boxing moves in *Rocky* and Jean-Claude Van Damme's karate kicks in *Street Fighter*. Obsessed with my heroes, I even told our friends that Gita and I were related to them. The kids believed me, at least for a while.

Every September, Mom and Dad applied for a US green card, and in May, a list of the selected people was posted. Gita and I would go with them to the city center and help them fill out the forms with our passport information, and we'd all pray that this time it would happen. We would be so excited and full of hope when we returned in the spring to check the list. But again and again, our names didn't appear, breaking our hearts a little more each time.

What was wrong with us? Why didn't we get chosen?

Still, Mom and Dad entered the lottery once again that fall. But given how unlikely it was that we'd be chosen, Dad kept looking for other ways to leave, especially as conditions worsened every day.

"I'm going to see Ali tonight," Dad told Mom one evening. "He wants to talk to me."

Ali Bregu, or Mr. Ali, as we called him, owned one of the largest, fanciest restaurants in Patos. Albanian by birth, he immigrated to Germany as a teenager and worked there for many years. After communism fell in the early 1990s, he returned home to Albania and used the money he managed to save to open his business.

It soon became a favorite among the wealthy. The entire area benefited. It made our town feel important and relevant, like we were connected to something bigger.

We visited the restaurant once when our cousin Durim had his wedding reception there. What an amazing place—large antique windows, modern light fixtures, big mirrors, and many beautiful paintings on the walls. The tables were covered with white linen, and the matching napkins folded at each place setting looked like roses.

After meeting Dad at the party, Mr. Ali often invited him to stop by for a drink. Mr. Ali knew people at the embassy, so when we overheard Dad tell Mom that he was going to see Mr. Ali, we thought he might be able to help us leave the country.

Years later, Dad told us that he and Ali sat outside at a corner table that night, in the balcony of the restaurant, gossiping over a beer.

There was little good news. The recent vandalism and violence had made the neighborhood dangerous. One of Ali's good friends had gotten shot in the head when he hesitated to hand over his wallet. Dad had met the man twice. He was young with a wife and three children. He had also been a good businessman.

This was one more reason Ali wanted to help us get out of the country. He always had the latest information about immigration, particularly to England. "What do you think, Gimi?" he said. "Do you want me to help you get to the UK?"

"Yes, absolutely," Dad said.

Ali shared all that he knew about cutting through the red tape in the immigration office. Not easy, he said. And a lot could go wrong with the various clandestine ways of immigration.

Dad listened carefully, wanting to make sure he understood all our options. He was about to ask a question when someone yelled from the far side of the restaurant. "Let me see you dance, boy! Dance for me. NOW!"

A man with short dark hair and a long beard stood on top of a chair pointing a gun, a Tokarev TT pistol, at Ladi, the young waiter, who had just served him a bottle of beer. Ladi cowered, trying to move away but the man was pointing the pistol at his head.

"I'm at work," Ladi said in a trembling voice. "I have many tables to serve. Please, let me be."

"Are you deaf, boy?" the man yelled. "Or do you have trouble listening to simple orders? I said dance or I'll put a bullet through your head!" He waved his pistol again in Ladi's face.

"You stupid, useless man. Aren't you listening to my friend?" another voice yelled out. A second man joined the first one at the table. He pulled out an AK-47 and pointed it at poor Ladi. "He said dance. Dance the Napoleon now!"

Seeing no other way out, poor Ladi started to mumble the song of the Napoleon, an Albanian traditional dance, and moved clumsily in front of the men.

"Ha!" The men laughed and shouted and then started banging

the table with forks, spoons, and glasses, trying to create a beat that Ladi could dance to.

Dad glanced over at Ali, who sat there pale and frozen. A block of a man, Ali had years of experience dealing with rowdy customers, yet he didn't move. All the other diners were paralyzed too. Dad felt sick, angry, and disgusted that Ladi, just a young kid, was the victim of these thugs' drunken games. Someone had to stop this. It had already gotten out of hand.

After taking a cursory look around the premises, Dad made up his mind. He pushed back his chair, making a loud scraping noise against the floor. Both men whipped around and pointed their guns at him.

"You! Sit down!" they yelled.

Dad couldn't help it—his courage left him. Faced with two guns pointed at his head, he sat down, his heart pounding as if he had run a marathon.

"Don't you like the waiter's performance?" the second man with the AK-47 said, sneering at Dad. "Why don't you come over here and dance for us? You can show us your moves. You're older than the waiter. You probably have more experience."

Both men howled with laughter.

Stay calm, Gimi, Dad told himself. *You can't deal with a drunk person pointing a gun at you.* He knew they were trying to goad him on, but it was better to ignore it.

"I'm sorry," he said once the laughter had died down. "I don't know how to dance at all."

"Ah, yes? Is that so?" The man with the AK-47 laughed. "We'll see if that's true." He climbed up on his chair, all the while waving his gun at Dad. "I want you to dance on top of the table. If you don't dance, I'll blow your brains out, and then, yes, you truly won't have any moves."

To punctuate his words, he fired his gun into the air in rapid fire three times. Several people screamed and ducked for cover.

Dad rose slowly to his feet. Keeping his voice even and controlled, he said, "Take it easy, young man. Let me leave and go home.

I'm sure you know many of my relatives—men like Berti and Nori Mustafaraj."

That should scare them. They would recognize those names—everyone who was anyone knew Berti and Nori. They didn't want to mess with either of them.

The armed man paused. "What's your relationship with Berti? I had a beer with him a week ago."

"I'm his brother-in-law, so let me go." Dad stood still, not taking his eyes off them as they whispered to each other.

The young man with the AK-47 cocked his head at him while he thought it over. "All right. Get the hell out of here before I change my mind."

As Dad backed away toward the exit, the young man climbed down from the chair. Using the tip of his gun, he started throwing all the silverware, glasses, and dishes onto the floor. The other man joined in as well.

Dad raced out to the sound of glass and china crashing. He felt so guilty leaving Mr. Ali alone. And he hadn't been able to help Ladi either, which weighed heavily on him.

The next day, Mr. Ali told Dad that the gangsters had left soon after he ran out. It was a miracle no one got hurt.

CHAPTER 6

Narrow Escapes

Deti

April 1998

One Saturday afternoon the following spring, Mom and Dad gave us permission to go into Patos for ice cream. It had been a while since any shootings had taken place, but they told us to come home right away.

"No dawdling," Mom said.

Excited, Gita and I walked into town. The sidewalks and streets were littered with debris and in bad need of repair. Some of the store windows shattered during the protests were still boarded up. Outside the ice cream shop, we bumped into two of our friends. I stayed with them while Gita went inside to buy a couple of cones.

The three of us were standing on the sidewalk talking when two young men in a red car pulled up to the curb. The guy in the passenger seat rolled down his window and asked my friends if they wanted to check out their car and go for a ride.

"No, thank you," they said. "We're eating our ice cream."

Seconds later, both men jumped out of the car and grabbed the girls by the shoulders. "Get in the car!"

The girls fought them, kicking and screaming, but the men shoved them into the back seat and slammed the door. Then one of the guys turned and started coming after me.

My heart in my throat, I bolted down the sidewalk. He was too big and fast for me. When he seized my wrist and yanked me to a stop, I bit his arm with everything I had. The metallic taste of blood filled my mouth. Swearing, he let go just as the other guy called out, "Leave her! We have to get out of here."

He ran back to the car and they sped off, the girls crying and screaming, banging on the windows to get out.

It happened so fast that Gita never saw anything. The girls were there one second and gone the next. All that was left was their smashed ice cream cones on the sidewalk.

I started shaking. Why hadn't anyone tried to stop them?

By the time we got home, I was sobbing uncontrollably and couldn't speak. Mom and Dad rushed to me, asking me what was wrong, and brought me over to the couch. Gita, in tears herself, told them the horrible story.

Mom put her arms around me and gently rocked me back and forth. "Deti, honey, you're safe now. We're right here," she whispered over and over again.

For days afterward, I couldn't eat or sleep. What if they came looking for me? Those men saw my face. I was afraid to go to school or even stand out on our balcony.

When I finally managed to go to sleep, I had nightmares that jolted me awake. Crawling into bed with Gita, she would hold me tight and tell me that everything was okay.

But I didn't believe her.

We had heard rumors about the sex-trafficking and prostitution rings in Patos, but now they were a reality we couldn't deny. More and more accounts of disappearing girls reached us. Those who escaped talked about the torture. If they refused to become prostitutes, their captors would extinguish cigarettes on their bodies or blindfold them and lock them in a box with only a small hole for air. Or the men would put a gun to their heads and threaten to kill them.

The gangs didn't always rely on kidnapping. In some cases, a man would pretend to be in love with a girl and treat her well for a few weeks. Then he would convince her to marry him and take her to Italy, where the girl would discover that it was all a lie.

Sadly, many Albanians, particularly older people, stigmatized the girls and women who managed to escape, as if they hadn't been held prisoner, as if somehow they had had a choice.

When our lives had first turned upside down more than a year before, I started giving Dad a hug every morning and asking him, "What time will you be home tonight?" I was afraid something might happen to him, that he'd be shot. After the girls were taken in town, I was terrified.

I needed to know where he was going every day and the exact time he'd be home. It annoyed him sometimes, but other times, he would laugh and tell me to stop acting like his mother.

When tears welled up in my eyes, he understood that my fears were getting the best of me. "I'll be home at nine o'clock, my angel. You can wait for me." He would kiss my forehead and tell me to have a good day at school.

As the spring turned to summer and the sky stayed lighter in the evening, the grown-ups sat on the steps of the apartment building, eating sunflower seeds and gossiping while the kids played in the courtyard. All the kids except me. I was up on the balcony watching for Dad.

The men used the same walkway when they came home from work. I watched each of them approach. Surely, the next man would be Dad. Or the next one or the one after him. I learned to identify each of the men from as far away as two hundred meters. Even when they were mere specks, I could tell, just from their shapes and the way they walked.

One night, the women were complaining again about Andon, our milkman. He was watering down the milk even more lately. It had always been fresh, thick, and creamy, but as times got harder, the quality started to change. Gita and I joked that the cows were poor now too.

The women agreed that Andon put in so much water that not
only did the milk taste bad, but the yogurt they made didn't turn out
right. The next time he made a delivery, they'd have to confront him
about it again, they said, though he would probably deny it as he
always did.

Just then, I spotted one of our neighbors and called down to the
man's wife, "Your husband is on his way home."

"Deti, child, how do you know that?" she asked.

"Because I can see him!" I pointed to a tiny dot in the distance.

Squinting, she looked where I was pointing and laughed. "What
are you talking about? I don't see anything."

"Wait and see." And sure enough, within a few minutes, her husband appeared on the walkway, approaching the apartments.

Whenever Dad was late, it was torture for me. If he said he would
be home by nine o'clock, I expected to see him by then. Slowly, the
minutes would tick by—9:05, 9:10. I got so scared I could barely
breathe.

And if it got to be twenty-five minutes after nine and Dad was
still not on the walkway, I couldn't hide my worry any longer, despite
wanting to. *Please, God, make him come home now. Let me see him on
the walk.*

"Deti, stop it!" Gita got so angry with me. "Why are you like this?
Stop crying. You're acting silly. You make everyone else feel bad with
all your worry." She always said that crying brought bad luck.

Gita seemed strong, but she was worried too. I could feel it. When
I asked her if Dad was on his way home, she would say she didn't
know. Her uncertainty made it worse. I couldn't rely on her protection anymore. I needed her to say everything was going to be
all right.

If Dad still wasn't home by our bedtime, I couldn't hold back the
tears any longer. "I can't go to bed," I told Mom. "I can't go to sleep
until Dad comes home."

"Don't worry, Deti," she said, hugging me and rubbing my back.
"He'll be home soon."

Mom would tuck us into bed, but that was when the intensive counting began. Every minute, I checked the clock. Soon it was ten o'clock. And then five after.

Sometimes I would play a game with myself. *He will be here by 10:15, and I will hear him open the door.* But 10:15 slowly became 10:20. I couldn't control the panic anymore and started crying.

Then suddenly, I heard someone on the staircase, someone coming up, coming closer. I recognized Dad's steps—I knew just how they sounded. And then I heard his voice. He was home!

I was so overjoyed, so relieved, that I wanted to jump out of bed and give him a big hug. I wanted to welcome him home and tell him how happy I was to see him and that I loved him so much. But I couldn't do that. I was supposed to be asleep. I had to lie in bed and keep all my feelings to myself. This evening my dad was safe.

On another night while I sat on the balcony anxiously waiting for Dad, I looked down and saw an ambulance in front of the apartment. Every part of me went dizzy with craziness. Was Dad inside?

When it started to drive away, I raced down the stairs and down the street, yelling, "Dad! Oh God, tell me it's not Dad!"

I chased the ambulance's flashing lights all the way to the hospital at the center of the city and then waited. I crossed my fingers. I prayed. Then the men opened the ambulance doors, and I moved closer to get a better look. They rolled out a stranger.

Thank you, God, thank you, thank you! The tears of relief came fast. Calming down, I looked around me. It was late, and I shouldn't have been out alone on the dark streets. What had I been thinking? I ran home and up the stairs.

Mom and Dad opened the door before I put my hand on the knob. Their faces were dark with anger. They had looked everywhere and couldn't find me. They were worried sick. I cried out of guilt now. I felt so ashamed.

Gita was furious too, but it didn't last long because she started to feel sorry for me.

"You must never do that again," Dad said, shaking his head.

"We're here to protect you," Mom said. "You don't have to protect us."

They thought they understood, but they didn't. How could I tell them about the fears that plagued my heart? Instead, I cried myself to sleep.

July 1998

Dad became even more determined to leave Albania. Again, we weren't selected in the US lottery, so he had to find another way. He talked to anyone who might be able to help.

One evening, he greeted us all with the biggest smile. "I have the best news. We're going to America!"

He swirled Mom around the kitchen as Gita and I jumped up and down, clapping our hands. Finally, our dreams would come true!

According to a private immigration group he had contacted, we would go by speedboat from Vlorë to Brindisi, Italy. From there, we'd take a train to Milan and then a plane to Philadelphia.

When Dad told Mom it would cost $15,000 for the trip, her face fell in disappointment. "Gimi, we don't have that kind of money."

Dad went on to say that he had talked to his good friend Nardi, who had received a green card and was now living in America. If we paid the initial $500 required to go to Brindisi, Nardi would loan us the remaining $14,500 when we arrived in Philadelphia. Dad had helped Nardi in the past, and he wanted to return the favor. Nardi would give us two years to repay the loan. Dad thought we could easily do that once we all had jobs.

The immigration group said they would have US passports and visas ready for us in Milan. Dad gave them the initial payment, and we started packing the few things we could take.

The hardest part was keeping it a secret from our friends and family. We told them we were going to the beach, never letting on we weren't coming back. No one could know the truth until we had reached the States.

We arrived in Vlorë at nine o'clock at night. A man met us on the dock and took an Instamatic photograph of all the passengers. He asked us to sign the back of it and wished us good luck with our journey. Later, we found out that because so many people didn't make it across the treacherous waters, they needed a record of everyone on board.

They crammed twenty of us into the small boat. It was actually a motorized rubber raft sitting low in the water, not the typical speedboat everyone had expected.

We were joined by two couples, a woman with her baby and two young children, and several young men. The pilot and copilot, two guys in their early thirties, bragged about how much experience they'd had taking their boat to Italy. They said we would make it in no time. A smooth, easy trip.

The copilot had only a few life jackets. He handed one each to Gita and me and the remaining three to the mother for herself and her kids. "We shouldn't have any problems," he said, "but if the water gets choppy, the rest of you can hold on to that." He pointed to the thick rope attached to the center of the boat on the inside.

We all sat huddled together on the bench seats, hanging on to our backpacks, our faces a mixture of wide eyes and nervous smiles. An hour later, we set off into the dark waters. Even though it was summer, the temperature dropped dramatically once we left the shore.

At first, the water was calm. But about a half hour in, the wind picked up and the waves started rocking the boat. In no time, the wind was roaring, and a huge wave came crashing down on us.

Everyone scrambled for the rope, pushing each other and screaming. Gita and I clung to Mom and Dad. Several of the passengers threw up over the side. We were all soaking wet.

Another monstrous wave pounded us and then another. The ruthless winds kept them coming, wall after wall of water engulfing us, the ocean showing no mercy.

With every wave, the woman with the children screamed, "We're going to die! We're going to die!" Over and over, she screamed.

One of the young men finally shouted at her, "Shut up! You're making it worse!"

And then another ferocious wave slammed against us.

Because everyone crowded around the rope, all the weight had shifted to one side of the boat. The copilot yelled, "We're going to tip over! Some of you must move to the other side."

"We aren't moving!" many of them said.

Several of the young men threw their bags into the water to help balance the boat. Dad held on to the very end of the rope and moved Mom, Gita, and me to the far side of the bench. He wrapped his arms and legs around me from behind, and Mom did the same with Gita.

The saltwater stung my eyes, and the wind scraped my face. I couldn't feel my fingers and toes. I'd never been so cold.

The closer we got to Italy, the faster the killer waves came. Surely, the next one would plunge us into the sea and our lives would end that very night.

"Dad, hold me!" I shouted. "Hold me!"

When it looked like Brindisi was within reach, a large boat pulled up alongside and shined a bright light at us. Border patrol. A man stood on the deck with a megaphone. "You must return!" he said in Italian. "It is far too dangerous to continue."

Several of us understood him and translated for the others. As the waves whipped our boat, the pilot shouted at the border patrol, "We can make it!"

"You have too many people on board. We can't help you. You must go back."

"Okay, okay." He nodded. "We'll go back."

Maybe there was hope for us after all.

The pilot turned the boat around, but as soon as the border patrol was out of sight, he resumed his original course. Everyone in the boat started screaming. The copilot pulled out an AK-47 and shot several times into the air. "Shut up or I'll kill you and throw you in the water!"

I looked at Mom and Dad and Gita, their eyes full of terror. Was this the choice we had? Drown in the icy water or be shot by these crazy men?

The pilot took us up and down the Brindisi coast, trying to break through the waves and get to shore. How could he risk our lives like that—including his own?

At last, the copilot yelled at him to stop and pushed him hard. The pilot pushed him back, his face distorted with rage. They punched each other as the waves battered us. Two of the young men grabbed the pilot and held him as the copilot turned the boat around.

By now, getting to America seemed like a distant dream. All that mattered was making it back to Albania alive.

I shivered violently. Would I ever be warm again?

When we reached the dock in Vlorë, everyone shoved their way out of the boat, desperate to get onto dry land. Dad gathered us in his arms, all of us shaking and sobbing with relief.

He hugged us tight. "God saved us. We'll keep trying, but from now on, we're taking a plane."

CHAPTER 7

Making New Plans

Deti

June 21, 1999

"Gimi!" Mom called out to Dad as soon as he walked through the door. "Kreshnik wants to see you. He has important news."

Kreshnik was our neighbor. Tall and thin, he was a quiet man of few words. He was married to Lavdie, his complete opposite—huge and loud. Every afternoon Lavdie would come over for a cup of Turkish coffee.

Earlier that day, Lavdie sat with Mom in the kitchen, her large body spilling over the sides of the chair and her booming voice filling our small apartment. She told Mom that Kreshnik's aunt asked him to come see her in Tirana right away. It was about visas for going abroad. "Gimi should go with him," Lavdie said.

Soon after our disastrous trip on the speedboat nearly a year before, Mom and Dad started talking about moving to Canada. They made plans with two of our second-floor neighbors. Mom and Dad said we would go by plane, with a regular visa, and arrive at Christmastime.

Since the holiday season was so busy, travel regulations would not be as strict as they normally were. For months, Gita and I lived this dream. Every night we prayed, counting down the days, until it was finally Christmas. But Christmas Day came and went and we still remained in Patos.

Dad said that he was so sorry, but the cost of the journey ended up being too high, coming to around $10,000 a person. Forty thousand dollars! We couldn't afford it at all. I cried for an entire week.

And then in May, we learned again that the US lottery hadn't come through for us. Meanwhile, violent gangs still controlled many parts of the country, and poverty was only getting worse.

Dad left immediately for Kreshnik's apartment on the fifth floor. Gita and I were already in bed, but we couldn't sleep. When we heard Dad's voice, we tiptoed to their door in the dark and caught parts of their conversation.

"Kreshnik's aunt lives next to a doctor who helps people emigrate," Dad said. "He has connections in Italy, Paris, the UK . . . I'll go tomorrow to find out more."

I hugged Gita. Maybe this was our answer.

The next morning, Mom told us that Dad was spending the night in Tirana. "We might have found someone who can get us to England."

Gita and I threw our arms around Mom. From everything we had learned about England at school, it was paradise compared to Albania.

On Wednesday afternoon, we were outside playing with our friends when we saw Dad coming up the walk into the courtyard. We ran to him, and he gave us both one of his special hugs. But something was wrong. I could see it in his eyes.

We followed him upstairs to our apartment. Mom opened the door before we even had a chance to turn the knob. "Did you meet him?" she blurted out. She was so anxious, she didn't even say hello to him.

"Oh my." Half smiling, Dad looked helplessly at Mom. "Let me take a shower and have dinner first. Then I'll tell you everything."

"Please, Gimi, tell us now. Go sit down. I'll get you a drink."

In the living room, we stood around Dad, crowding close as he dropped onto the couch and took a sip of his whiskey.

"I think this group is serious," he said. "The journey isn't long. We can travel by plane, and they'll give us legal visas."

Mom bent down and hugged Dad. "Wonderful. Let's leave at once!"

He shook his head. "There's only one problem . . ."

"Yes? Yes?" Mom said impatiently.

"It will cost $12,000, and we have to pay them in three days."

"Is that all?" I said, hands on my hips, grinning broadly. "We can borrow the money, Dad!"

Freedom, safety, and a beautiful world—a chance to leave Albania and go to England. That would be the very best present in the world!

"That's a lot of money," Mom said. She fell silent and started pacing the room. "But we can do it. Borrow $5,000 from my cousin Lui and $3,000 from your relatives, and we already have $4,000 saved."

Dad put down his drink and stared at Mom. "We have $4,000, Dita?"

Gita and I grinned at each other. Mom was a thrifty woman, always thinking about saving for an emergency like this. But what we also loved about her was her pushiness. She wouldn't give Dad a moment of rest until we had the money and we were on our way.

"See if you can talk with Lui tomorrow," Mom said. "And then on Friday, you can meet with your relatives and ask them for help."

In bed that night, I prayed to God and thanked him. It felt like he had finally answered all my prayers and we would be leaving Albania soon.

An amazing movie played in my imagination. I was inside a different world. I could smell the freshness of the air, making the freedom and peace of the UK all the more refreshing. I could smile without fear. I was free of worries and couldn't care less about when my dad was coming home because I knew he would always be safe. As a family, we did many things together, like visiting parks, reveling among the colorful flowers that radiated with the joy I felt. I had a pink bike I rode every weekend racing Gita and brand-new white trainers for soccer.

And there were no guns. I drifted off into a delicious sleep.

The next day, Mom shared her plans with Lavdie.

"You see? I knew it!" Lavdie said. "What did I tell you? You would find a way because every time I read your coffee cup, I get the same answer. Your road is long and white!"

Whenever Mom and Lavdie had a cup of Turkish coffee together, they read their futures in the coffee grounds. After Lavdie went home, Gita and I would have great fun imitating her. We had her script down pat.

"I see a number five in your cup," Gita would say, pretending to be Lavdie while I pretended to be Mom. She tried to keep a straight face but always started giggling. "Make a wish," she'd say.

I would close my eyes.

"Your wish will come true. I see a white horse. Yes, you're riding a white horse!"

By now, we would be laughing so hard, we couldn't go on. Lavdie said that when you saw a white horse in the coffee grounds, it was a blessing and good fortune.

The fortune telling was silly, but we knew it gave Lavdie and Mom hope. They weren't alone in wanting to leave Albania as quickly as possible. Most of our neighbors were trying to find a way out, and they did whatever they could to lift one another's spirits.

That day, Lavdie was beaming. "As soon as we give the money to the doctor, we can leave. It should take only a week for the visas."

Mom eyed her friend anxiously. "Lavdie, tell me honestly. Don't you think $12,000 is too much money?"

"Not at all. That's a reasonable price for a safe trip. You can pay less in advance and travel by boat to Italy, like you did last year. But you know how dangerous that was. And you heard about the speedboat that sank last week and all the people died? Do what you think is best for you and your family, but my husband is going to give the money to the doctor tomorrow."

Mom pressed her lips together and frowned. Reaching over, Lavdie patted her hand. "It will work out, Dita. You've always been lucky."

CHAPTER 8

Nip and Tuck

Gita

June 24, 1999

"There he is!" Deti said, pointing.

She and I had just gotten home from school and were on the balcony watching for Dad. He met with Cousin Lui that morning to ask about borrowing money. Lui had worked in Switzerland for close to five years and made hundreds of thousands in Swiss francs. No one knew how. Everyone assumed he would spend most of his life there, thinking he was living like a king, but he shocked all of us by returning to Albania for good.

We greeted Dad at the door, and he leaned down to hug us. He called us angels, like he always did, but he wasn't smiling.

My heart sank.

Mom was in the kitchen cooking. She gave us a look, and we got the message to leave them alone, but we needed to find out what had happened. We hid by the doorway so we could hear.

"Lui said he loaned money to other people a week ago, and he can help us after they pay him back," Dad said with a sigh.

"Damn him! I know he has the money. What are we going to do? Don't tell me you believed his silly reason?"

"Of course not. We both know Lui too well. He turned us down because he doesn't want us to leave. He is basing everything on his past experiences."

Past experiences? What was he talking about?

I remembered Lui saying once that he had witnessed many horrific events in Switzerland, some of which involved teenagers being kidnapped and sold to handlers. But what did that have to do with us?

"Lui's crazy," Mom said. "He goes on about his and others people's experiences in Switzerland, but he has no idea what it's been like living in this country with children. We are all lucky to be alive, and things will only get worse. Why does he have to be so stubborn? I know he has the money."

They were quiet for a moment and then Mom said, "Gimi, I promise you, I'll find a way to get that $5,000."

Deti's eyes filled with tears. I felt crushed too. But Mom's promise gave me hope. When she set her mind to do something, no one could stop her.

"It's going to work, Deti," I whispered, wiping away her tears with the back of my hand. "I know it."

Later that evening, Lavdie and Kreshnik came by with their two children. Maybe they figured out a way to help us so we could leave together.

"We've already started packing our things," Lavdie said. "We want to be ready to go when our visas come."

Kreshnik put his hand on Dad's shoulder. "Gimi, find the money as soon as you can. We'd really like you to join us, but we can't wait and risk it."

"Of course, you should go," Dad said, his voice heavy with disappointment. "And may God help you on your trip."

Kreshnik nodded. "Okay, then." He glanced at Mom and then at Deti and me. "I'll meet the doctor tomorrow."

"Please tell him I'm still interested. I'll find a way to get the money."

After Kreshnik and his family left, Mom whipped around, her eyes blazing. "Gimi, why did you tell him not to wait for us a little longer? Now, they will leave and we'll be stuck here in Albania! You shouldn't have said that!" She marched around the living room, wringing her hands.

"Calm down, Dita, calm down! I'll talk to the doctor to see if we can arrange something. Maybe we can give him half the money now and the rest of it later. If that's the case, I'll also give him our passports and ask him to give us visas."

Before we went to bed, Deti and I stood out on the balcony, looking up at the open, endless sky, and prayed together with every bit of strength we had. Surely Jesus or Mother Mary would help us.

Kreshnik stopped by again the next evening to talk to Dad. Mom shooed us into our bedroom, but as soon as she left, we crept out into the hallway to listen.

"The doctor said he wants the money from us within a week," Kreshnik said. "He can't wait any longer. There are too many Albanians who already have $12,000. If you can't get the money this week, you'll have to wait until December to leave."

"I have an appointment with the doctor tomorrow," Dad said. "I'll ask him if he's willing to accept our passports with $6,000 now, and then we'll pay the balance when our visas are issued."

"I don't know, Gimi, he seemed pretty firm on this." Kreshnik paused. "But maybe you'll get lucky. It's worth a shot."

Later, when Dad came into our bedroom to say good night, we pretended that we hadn't heard anything. Even when he told us about going to Tirana early in the morning, we didn't ask any questions despite the tension in his voice. Instead, we talked about Grandma Lira and Grandpa Llazi, his parents. He was going to visit his parents in Bubullimë on his way back from Tirana.

The next day, Deti and I couldn't sit still. We kept a sharp watch for Dad all afternoon, searching for him throughout the neighborhood. When it got dark, we stationed ourselves back on the balcony. Finally, framed in the lights of a nearby store was the familiar silhouette of a man approaching. We raced down the stairs to meet Dad, each of us trying to be the first to hug him and help him carry the bags of groceries he brought from our grandparents' village.

I reached him first. Putting down his bags, he laughed heartily and wrapped his arms around me and then Deti. He was hot and sweaty but oh so happy. He must have good news! I tried to lift one of the bags. "Deti, this is too heavy. Help me."

She placed her hands under one side of the bag, and we carried it between us back to the apartment. Mom hadn't finished her coffee meeting at Lavdie's flat, so Dad decided to take a shower. Deti and I quickly set to work unpacking the groceries. I dug down into the heavy bag and found a large watermelon. As I pulled it out, I saw a small blue packet underneath.

"What's in it?" Deti asked.

I opened it. Inside was another packet. A white one—full of cash.

Deti's eyes grew wide with excitement. "Is that what I think it is?"

"Dad has solved the problem," I whispered. "We can go to England!"

"Yes, yes!" Deti jumped up and down and started to whirl around in circles like a happy puppy, dragging me with her.

Suddenly I pulled her to a stop. Footsteps on the stairs. "Mom's coming."

Deti hurried to the table and put the packet and watermelon back into the bag. "Pretend like you're stacking the vegetables to wash them."

I got busy just as Mom walked through the door. "Where's Dad?" she asked, seeing the groceries.

He appeared in the doorway. "Right here," he said, refreshed from his shower.

Mom rushed over to greet him. "How did it go, Gimi? Do you have news?" She was so anxious for answers that she forgot Deti and I were there.

Dad smiled. "It went better than expected. Much, much better. My relatives in the village let me borrow $4,000!"

Mom's hands flew to her mouth. "Really?"

"Yes! And do you want to know the best part?" He squeezed her shoulders. "They didn't give me a deadline for returning the money. Do you know what that means? No pressure in repaying. And I'm not done—there's something else."

"What?" Mom asked breathlessly.

"The doctor has agreed to accept half the money now and promised that he'd do everything he could to issue us the visas as soon as possible."

"Really? Oh my God!" Mom threw her arms around Dad. Then she pulled away and became serious again. "So now we have $8,000 and we need $4,000 to seal the deal. Maybe we could borrow the money from Durim?"

Mom's nephew, the son of her oldest brother, Kutbi, was well off. Durim had lived in Greece for eight years, and was now working with his brother to build a store at the city center. Dad agreed with Mom, saying that he had already been thinking about that.

In the morning, he set out to meet Durim at the store.

Two days later, as Deti and I were walking home from school, we spotted our sweet Uncle Kutbi laboring up the hill that led into our neighborhood. He had health problems and didn't visit us often. By the time he reached the top of the hill, he was already winded.

"Hello my lovely nieces," he said, panting and smiling broadly at us. "I'm all sweaty—don't kiss me!"

Deti and I paid no attention to him and planted several kisses on his face.

"This is for you." He handed us a white plastic bag.

My eyes opened wide at the sight of the chocolates and bananas. I couldn't remember the last time I had eaten a banana. They weren't available in Patos until 1995, but they were very expensive. A small banana could easily cost around 250 lek. We ate our first one a couple of years before, when Mom bought it in the market at Fier. It tasted weird. The second banana we had a few months later was much better. Since then, every time we had one, we ate each bite slowly to make it last longer.

We couldn't accept any of the treats from Uncle Kutbi—at least not yet. Mom always told us that we needed to refuse our relatives' gifts so they wouldn't spend money on us the next time. Deti and I had to first pretend that we didn't want the bananas or the chocolates.

Then Uncle Kutbi would insist and get upset, so to make him happy, we would pretend that we were accepting the gifts.

"Thank you, Uncle! We love you."

He didn't come just to give us bananas and chocolates. His visit had something to do with the remaining money. We followed him up to our apartment, resting with him on the banister so that he could catch his breath.

Despite his fatigue, Uncle Kutbi stayed standing once he came inside. "I brought you the money, Gimi," he said.

Mom and Dad both rose from the couch and stood immobile, speechless, almost like statues.

Uncle Kutbi looked back and forth between them. "Never forget that you are very dear to me. You've made a big decision. I hope it's a good one. May God help you . . ." His voice broke, and he couldn't continue.

Dad gave him a big, strong hug, like one you would give to your best friend. "Thank you. It's because of you that Durim gave us the money. It's unbelievable."

He started laughing, laughing like I hadn't seen him laugh before, lifting me up in the air, whirling me around. Mom's eyes shone with happy tears.

Now all Dad had to do was book another appointment with the doctor.

CHAPTER 9

Snags and Secrets

Gita

July 12, 1999

Dad sat on the couch and took a few sips of water as Deti, Mom, and I gathered around him. Then he put down the glass and began.

"When I saw the doctor today, I met two other guys who belong to the group that makes all the arrangements for the trip to the UK. They'll issue us a two-week short-stay Schengen visa and—"

"What's a Schengen visa?" Deti interrupted.

I pulled on her hand to stop her from asking questions. Mom and Dad had finally let us become a part of the conversation about the trip, but I could tell there were still things they didn't want us to hear. If we asked a lot of questions, we might remind them that we weren't adults. Deti pushed my hand away and gave me a dirty look.

"It's a document that gives us permission to travel freely in all states in Schengen," Dad said.

Deti pretended to understand, but I knew she was still clueless. Yet she couldn't ask another question, so I took the risk. "Schengen countries are like Italy, France, Austria, and Belgium?"

Dad nodded. "That's right."

Deti patted my shoulder. I couldn't tell whether she was proud of me or happy that she got the answer to one of her own questions.

"Two weeks isn't a long time for a visa," Mom said, frowning.

"But it doesn't take anywhere near two weeks to go to England. Right, Dad?" Deti said.

"And what about the money?" Mom said. "Will we get it all back if we don't make it?"

I held my breath. Twelve thousand dollars was a lot of money to pay back if we didn't get to the UK. How on earth would Mom and Dad be able to save that much money in Albania?

"I already asked all those questions and they assured me that everything would be okay," Dad said. "It's a hundred percent guaranteed."

Guaranteed. What did that really mean, once we left Albania? How could they tell Dad anything was guaranteed in times like these?

"Did the doctor tell you this or one of the other men?" Mom asked.

"It was Edi, not the doctor. He's the head of the group. In his fifties, I'd say. Seems like the kind of guy you wouldn't want to pick a fight with."

"And what did he say exactly?"

"That he understood our situation. Since he's ex-military, being straight with people is a rule he has followed all his life. Edi introduced me to his nephew, Mateo, who has contacts with the embassy of a western European country. Mateo said that the visas are authentic, but I'd have to follow all the regulation procedures perfectly to get them."

Dad took another sip of water and put down the glass. "That's not all."

Mom raised her eyebrows impatiently. "Yes, Gimi?"

"Both Edi and Mateo agreed not to take the rest of the money until we arrived safely in England. The doctor told them that they were dealing with an honest, rational man. Once we reach our destination safely, one of our relatives will bring the money to them."

"Ah, now that's much better." Mom's face brightened.

Dad smiled. "Yes, I admit, it makes the whole deal seem more secure."

"He trusts you."

Dad looked at Mom, Deti, and me. "This time we're going to make it."

"This time" felt different—more real and also very scary. Our dream wasn't going to vanish again. Dad's optimism was contagious. And Mom? I had never seen her act like this before. She was laughing for no reason. It was really happening!

I was already dreaming of the fragrant green fields, the beautiful bicycle, the new school we would go to, and the cool schoolbags Deti and I would have, with plenty of pockets to carry everything. We would finally have everything we desired once we got to the UK, like the many, many colored pens and pencils in all the shades of the rainbow.

I pictured what it would be like when we arrived. Deti and I would go to London, visit Big Ben, the same one that we read about in English class with Mrs. Alma. And our English—oh, it would be massively improved. I'd be able to speak like a proper English lady, and when I returned to Albania, I could show off to my friends.

Deti hugged me. I felt her joy. No words needed to pass between us. We both knew *this time* we were on the right track.

Three days later, when a pickup truck pulled up in front of our apartment building, I stopped my game with my friends and ran to get Deti. "Isn't that Uncle Berti?" The man stepping out of the truck looked familiar—dark, tall, and skinny. Yes, it was him.

"Uncle Berti!" We ran to him. He hugged us both at the same time, but he didn't lift us up in the air the way he usually did. He seemed preoccupied and distant.

"Is something wrong, Uncle?" I asked him.

"No, no." He smiled at us. "But I have to go see your mom."

Deti and I knew better than to follow him up to the apartment. When we saw his truck leave, we bounded up the stairs. Mom was briskly scrubbing the floor. The caustic fumes of bleach filled the air. Up and down, back and forth she scrubbed. Something bad must have happened.

Mom didn't say a word. She didn't even look up at us. Deti and I went into the living room and turned on the TV, waiting for Mom to finish cleaning, waiting for her to tell us—*what?*

My heart pounded. I couldn't focus on the screen. Deti sat up straight, alert. Then came Dad's footsteps, soft on the stairs, light as a feather. Deti jumped up from the sofa, and I followed her into the kitchen.

Mom was squeezing out the cleaning rag when Dad came through the door and bent down to take off his shoes. "Finally, Gimi! Berti was here, and he told me to tell you to call the doctor."

Dad straightened up right away, blinking at Mom. "Did he say why?"

"No. He wouldn't tell me."

"I'll go next door to the Brakas' and call him at once."

He turned and vanished. A lump rose to my throat. Deti and I both stared at Mom, who has never been able to hide her emotions well. Her green eyes, usually soft and warm, grew dark and flickered from anxiety to anger and finally to despair.

"It's okay, Deti," I said in a low voice. "We'll find out what's going on soon. Everything will be fine."

Yet I knew my words wouldn't comfort her. How could they? She looked at me, her face clouded with fear, and then she focused on the clock on the wall. We both watched the second hand tick by. Its movement was somehow soothing, showing a purpose and strength in pushing through time.

Soundlessly, as if he were a ghost, Dad swept back into the apartment, and we jumped in unison. He was grinning broadly. Deti glanced at me as if to confirm what she was seeing.

"Listen to this," Dad said, his voice filled with excitement. "The doctor says Mom and I need to go to the embassy tomorrow to be interviewed for the Schengen visas."

"Yay!" Deti screamed, waving her hands up in the air.

Mom's mouth dropped. I had never felt so terrified, so elated, so totally overcome with joy.

We found out that the doctor had called Dad's office at Albeptrol and left a message with one of the employees. Miraculously, Uncle Berti happened to meet the employee at a coffee shop. Nothing was easy in Albania then. Without cell phones or a landline, we might as well have been living in the Dark Ages. Yet Patos was a small town. Everyone knew everyone and word spread fast.

I pressed my hands together. They were so cold, I was so cold, so scared inside that it might not be true. But it was true. Then, as if to reassure me, Deti nodded and yelled again, "Yay!"

Yes, at last it was really true. In a few days we could have visas to travel to the UK. Most people waited months to get a visa. Kreshnik and Lavdie were still waiting for theirs, and they started the process weeks before.

I let out a little giggle. We must be lucky. At least luckier than Kreshnik and Lavdie. Lavdie's coffee grounds. Mom's good fortune that Lavdie had predicted.

Later that night, as Dad hugged and kissed us good night, he grew serious. "I want to remind you that we need to keep this a secret. No one else can know that we may be going to England. You can't say a word to anyone."

This was so unfair it hurt. "Couldn't we make an exception this time?" I asked.

He shook his head. "No one but our closest friends and relatives. This is very important. Do you understand?" Dad waited for us to meet his eyes. "Do you promise?"

"I promise," Deti said.

"Yes, I promise," I echoed, biting my lip and nodding.

My thoughts were racing all over the place, and I knew Deti's were too. Why did adults exaggerate things when they spoke to children? Perhaps I'd be able to answer that question when I was an adult myself.

Tomorrow I would have to pretend that we had no plans for leaving Albania, that I would never leave my friends. We had kept secrets before, but somehow this seemed more real, more final.

As soon as Dad closed our bedroom door behind him, Deti turned to me. "Gita." Her eyes welled with tears. I couldn't let her sleep alone. I got into her bed and held her tightly, feeling her fear or sadness or whatever it was that hid deep within her and in me. I could feel her tears falling. All my pent-up sadness spilled out too, breaking my shield of pretending to be strong. Deti's warm tears blended with mine.

"How can we leave without saying goodbye to our friends?" she said.

"Deti, they'll understand."

"They'll have to." She sobbed.

By morning the storm had passed. I slept soundly and woke up feeling refreshed. I didn't think about the secret and the promise to Dad. When I opened my eyes, I remembered only my beautiful dream.

I was at an English school. It was large, modern, and clean. The desks were so comfy. On the first day, the head teacher gave Deti and me large school bags with rulers and pencils and pens. We had geography, but there was no large map on the white board and I couldn't see Mrs. Nat anywhere.

Of course not. Mrs. Nat was back in Albania. The British teacher was chubby with curly hair. She gave me a small map and told me to color the countries using the different colored pencils the head teacher had given me. It was easy. I felt no pressure, and although I was shy, I made a few friends. Everyone was polite. I liked them—but I still sat with Deti.

It was just a dream, though.

When I went out to the living room, Lefta, Mr. Braka's daughter, was sitting on the sofa, sipping coffee. Our "big sister" looked over at me with her big brown eyes and smiled. "Good morning. Your mom and dad left a couple of hours ago." Breakfast was waiting for us on the table: slices of homemade bread with butter and jam and a glass of milk.

I gave Deti a gentle nudge to wake her up. We needed to spend as much time as we could with Lefta. Lately, we'd been feeling annoyed at her for getting engaged to Axhem, a handsome young man who moved to the UK. I told Lefta that her fiancé looked like a prince.

But I didn't really mean it. I said it only to make her happy. What hurt most was that she still hadn't introduced him to us. Who was the guy stealing our Lefta from us? She had been all ours for twelve whole years. Until a few months before, Lefta used to tell us fairy tales and paint our nails for us. But now she seemed changed.

She no longer paid attention to Deti and me. Her mind was somewhere else. She talked to the women a lot more. I had overheard Mom saying that Lefta was planning to join Axhem, but I didn't ask Lefta about it because I didn't want to hear her answer. If she left Albania, that meant she would abandon us.

Lefta didn't know that Deti and I had cried over the thought of losing her. Every day we would run home from school to ask her father whether she'd left Albania yet.

But now that we might be going to England ourselves, we didn't have to torment ourselves over Lefta leaving us anymore. Yes, I was sure Lefta would remain ours forever, whether Axhem was near or far.

In the afternoon, as soon as we heard footsteps on the staircase, we ran to the door to meet Mom and Dad. They waited until Lefta went home before they said anything.

"It's good and not so good," Mom said, holding us close. "The embassy issued Dad and me a two-week business Schengen visa. The problem is with your visas. Mateo promised Dad that he would get around it by putting your names on mine. But he'll need a few days to do that..." Her voice trailed off. She was tired and doubtful again.

"Will that work, Dad?" I asked quietly.

Dad shrugged, offering no assurances. I didn't dare ask any more questions.

"We have to pray harder," Deti said resolutely.

The next six days passed slowly. Mom shared everything with us, trying to keep our spirits up, yet we were all worried. Pretending that everything was okay was impossible. Mateo still hadn't solved the problem of visas for Deti and me, and in just a little over a week,

Mom's and Dad's visas would expire. If that happened, they would have to go through the same process to get them renewed. And then who knew how long we'd have to wait.

On the seventh day, Dad burst through the door. "Girls, the group has fixed the problem. As Mateo said, you two and Mom will use one visa. And . . . we're leaving the day after tomorrow."

"The day after tomorrow!" the three of us shouted. My head began to spin. I felt scared and excited all at once. I reached out for Deti's hand. It was as cold as mine.

We had no time to think. We followed Mom around the apartment as she frantically packed everything on her list. Then we needed to find someone who would give us a ride to Tirana.

We had to choose the best clothes to take with us. It was heartbreaking that I couldn't give my best friend, Jonida, the clothes I had to leave behind. I felt like I was betraying her. I was overcome by a wave of uncertainty. Our dream was finally coming true, and I felt sad. Why was that?

Soon I would know what it was like to live in a country far away from Albania. When I was ten years old, the father of our classmate Dritan worked in Germany. One day his father sent him a pair of Adidas trainers, a Power Ranger school bag, a large eraser, and a blue compass. He told everyone about his new treasures, and we all crowded around his bench to check them out.

Dritan took on an importance in the class. Although he wasn't bright, he was well-respected and I envied his gifts. Deep inside, I wished the school bag and pens belonged to me. But now, was this what I really wanted? Suddenly, everything was happening too fast.

"We have to go see Grandma Lako," I said. Deti agreed.

"Of course," Mom said. "We'll visit Grandma tomorrow." She sat down and then stood again, wiping the back of her hand across her forehead. She pulled each of us close and stroked our hair as if to calm herself.

Her mother, our grandma Lako, was one of the most important people in our lives, and lately she hadn't been well. She had high blood pressure and several other physical problems. Once we left Albania, we might never see her again.

I had a hard time falling asleep that night. When I looked over at Deti, I saw that I wasn't the only one. I sensed that she, too, was being bombarded by thoughts, a million questions and doubts, with no answers and more uncertainty.

I stretched out my hand to touch hers.

CHAPTER 10

Farewells

Gita

July 23–24, 1999

The next morning, we walked along the side of the road to Grandma Lako's house. That walk was different from all the others. I paid attention to everything and realized how beautiful our little town was. I had been blind not to have noticed it before. With love and a little regret, I drank in the flowers, the grass, the trees, every little detail.

This was my last day in Patos. So I really needed to make sure I remembered everything.

Coming toward us was Kristina. Petite with short black hair, she was always loud and happy. For our first four years in primary school, Kristina was our teacher and tutor. She and Mom had become friends. After we started secondary school, we didn't see her much anymore. But the strong relationship was always there. Today, God sent her just at the right moment. It was bittersweet to see her one last time.

I wanted to tell her we were leaving. It was so hard to keep the news to myself. Kristina wished us goodbye, saying she would see us later, but we would already be on our way to England by then.

As we entered the house, Grandma Lako heard us and called out cheerfully from her bedroom. "I'm in bed. Oh, I feel so much better now that you're here." We hugged and kissed her tenderly. Her wonderful smile never left her face.

Mom's sister-in-law, Auntie Dhurata, who lived with Grandma

Lako, was on the balcony outside, and in the distance, I could see Uncle Nori and Cousin Bushi gathering grapes from the vines and placing several bunches in a large white bowl. Mom sat with Auntie Dhurata and had their usual coffee.

Deti and I stayed with Grandma Lako and chattered with her about our friends, our school, about anything we could think of besides what was really going on in our minds. She mixed us up, like most of our family did, but we didn't stop to correct her.

Our beloved Grandpa Baba had been gone for five years by then. He and Grandma Lako had raised five daughters and five sons. They had also buried a son and daughter, so they weren't strangers to suffering. One of their sons died of hypothermia while exploring the countryside, and their youngest daughter fell down a well at the age of four.

Following the death of her two children, Grandma Lako had another son she named Dalan, after her son who died, and then another daughter she named Afërdita, or Dita, our mom, after her daughter who had died so young.

All too soon it was time for Grandma Lako to take her medications and for us to leave. As she dozed off, I secretly wiped away my tears. Nobody saw me but Deti, who started crying too.

We kissed Grandma softly on her forehead. Just as we turned to go, she opened her eyes. "Why are you leaving so early? Stay here with me." She probably sensed something.

"Gimi forgot his house key and might come home any moment," Mom said, a tremor in her voice.

And then Grandma asked to kiss our hands one last time.

Leaving her made my heart heavy, and I could barely move my feet. But it was Mom who found it so hard to close the front door. She kept looking over her shoulder as we walked away.

Grandma's little black dog, Xebi, followed us. He had never done that before. Even Xebi must have sensed something was happening. We couldn't see Grandma's house anymore. Mom began crying loudly. She fumbled in her bag for a handkerchief, and soon it was drenched with her tears. Wordlessly Deti and I placed an arm around her waist.

"Mom, you'll see Grandma Lako again," I said. "You will."

The truth was, I didn't know if any of us would ever see Grandma Lako again.

Xebi was still following us. I motioned to him and told him in so many different ways that he couldn't come with us, but he wagged his tail stubbornly and refused to turn around.

Deti stroked his back and he finally understood and trotted off in the direction of Grandma's house. After we got home, Mom kept crying, and we didn't know how to help her. Deti and I were sitting on the sofa in front of the TV without turning it on, completely consumed by our sadness, when the door opened and in walked Uncle Berti, Auntie Ani, and our cousins Frida, Lela, and Erion, or little Rocky, as we called him, because he resembled Sylvester Stallone in the Rocky Balboa movies.

Their presence lit up the room. They were among the few who knew we were leaving and they wanted to say goodbye. But that night, even our cousins weren't energetic. Their smiles were forced, their sorrow visible in their eyes. Uncle Berti's greeting was short and cold as if he wanted to avoid us. He sat on the sofa smoking a cigarette, lost in his thoughts.

Auntie Ani broke the silence. "What's up with all the sad faces?" she said. "We have no time to be sad. We have things to do. Suitcases to be packed. What are you planning to take with you?"

Deti and I told her we were taking our best clothes, as Mom said.

Auntie Ani handed us a white box. "I have something for you girls."

Deti and I removed the lid. Inside was a small figurine of Mother Mary.

"Oh, Auntie Ani!" We both looked at her, our eyes shining with tears. "Thank you. You couldn't have given us a better gift."

She held us close. "Mother Mary will protect you. You'll have a safe journey and so much good luck. God will bless you, and you'll have everything you've been wishing for."

Deti and I took turns holding the beautiful white figurine. "The Virgin Mary will be with us wherever we go."

Uncle Berti rose to his feet and said it was time to leave, but our cousins wanted to stay the night. "Please, Dad?" they all said at once. He looked at all five of us kids and nodded, smiling. How could he refuse such a request?

Before we went to bed, I gave Frida my gold pendant with the letter "A" that my parents bought me for my tenth birthday, and she placed her gold pendant with the initial "F" around my neck. That way we would be with each other every minute.

This was now my greatest treasure.

We slept so soundly that we didn't hear Uncle Berti's footsteps on the stairs when he arrived. And we didn't hear Mom either until she was shaking us awake, telling us it was time to get dressed. Part of me didn't want to wake up because that meant having to say goodbye and enduring a final separation from our loving cousins. Frida wouldn't open her eyes. She covered her head with a blanket and burst into tears when Deti pulled it down.

Uncle Berti would take our cousins home first and then come back to drive us to Tirana. As we waited, Deti and I walked silently through the apartment, carefully studying every nook and cranny as if memorizing it. We had lived in that house for close to thirteen years. That's all we knew.

It had taken so long for us to find a way to leave Albania, and now that the moment had finally arrived, everything was happening too fast. It felt unfair, being forced to let go of all the people and things we loved.

"Girls! Uncle Berti is waiting," Dad called from the kitchen. "Come on, let's go."

Turning our backs on our home, on our room, on all of our possessions, we forgot to kiss our beautiful dolls goodbye. Aglenda and Rozalba had meant so much to us for many years.

We closed the front door and tiptoed down the stairs to make sure no one heard us leaving. Deti and I counted the steps one last time. "Forty-nine, forty-eight, forty-seven." Years before, we had carved our initials on number forty-six. We had climbed up and down those stairs thousands of times, ever since we could walk. They would always have our footprints.

As sad as I was about leaving, a part of me also felt important. We weren't going to stay in Albania like everyone else. Our lives would be different. So much better. We were going to England!

Uncle Berti's gray Mercedes was waiting. My eyes stung with tears. *Goodbye, home. Goodbye, everything I love. I will miss you . . .*

Mom pulled us into the car and Uncle Berti pressed his foot on the gas pedal. We stared out of the window, looking back at our neighborhood until the car turned and we couldn't see it anymore.

We were truly on our way. Uncle Berti accelerated as we drove onto the main highway. He was quiet, probably worried and nervous like the rest of us. We were all absorbed in our own thoughts, asking the same questions over and over. At some point, I must have fallen asleep because the next thing I knew we were in Tirana.

We arrived at the doctor's house ten minutes late. He was outside, pacing in the driveway. As soon as our car stopped, he held up his hand, signaling for us to follow him in his own car.

At the Café Tirana, the doctor drove off, and we went inside, where Edi and his nephew, Mateo, were waiting for us. "Would you like something to drink?" Edi asked after greeting us.

We took a seat on the balcony. The warm breeze tousled my hair, and it seemed like an ordinary summer day. But it was far from ordinary.

The waiter placed three espressos in front of Mom, Dad, and Uncle Berti and returned with lemonade for Deti and me. No one spoke, an uneasiness filling the air. Uncle Berti consumed his entire cup of espresso in one gulp, as if it were nasty medicine he had to get down.

Edi, seated opposite, looked at me and then at Deti. "So which one is which?"

"I have a mole on my right cheek," Deti said.

"You must be the older one."

Deti giggled. "Practically, the youngest, theoretically, the oldest, because Gita does what I say."

Mom placed an arm around my shoulder, squeezing me tightly, and smiled proudly at each of us. Edi asked the next predictable question, "Which one of you is better in school?"

I pinched Deti to get her attention, but she already knew what I was going to say. "I hope Mom doesn't show off this time," she whispered.

"Impossible," I whispered back.

Mom's smile broadened. "They are both bright and do very well in school. They also take private English lessons."

Deti stepped on my foot to tell me that Mom said exactly what she predicted she would say. It was all so embarrassing.

Before Edi could ask another question, Mateo broke his silence. "Well, are you ready?"

"Yes, we're ready . . . ," Dad said with uncertainty in his voice.

Mateo didn't respond. Lighting a cigarette, he tilted his head back and blew the smoke toward the sky. Then slowly, deliberately, he placed the cigarette on the edge of the ashtray.

"There's only one change," he said calmly.

"A change?" Dad leaned forward, his eyes narrowing.

Edi took over for Mateo. "You aren't going by plane. You'll be traveling another way."

Uncle Berti flew out of his chair and pounded on the plastic table. "What the hell are you talking about?"

"You told us we would go by plane," Dad said frostily.

Edi motioned for Uncle Berti to sit down. "Come on, men, don't worry. This other way is safe too, and there will be no problems. It's just that it will take more time. You must understand that things aren't simple. All the people who have traveled by plane were turned back in Italy because it was obvious they wanted to emigrate. We can't risk that."

"So I suppose the promise of the plane was simply to lure us, and we'll be traveling by speedboat after all." Dad glared first at Edi and then at Mateo. "I made it clear that we never wanted to travel by speedboat."

Deti looked at me in horror. If Dad decided we weren't going, Edi and Mateo might get into a fight with Dad and Uncle Berti and get them killed.

I flashed back to something I had witnessed the previous summer when we went to Divjaka Beach with Uncle Berti and his family. Due to water problems, people had to get their water from a communal pump, and there was always a long line in front of it. Two neighbors fought over which person was first, and they ended up killing each other. The discussion between Mateo and Dad was much more important, much bigger. And the times we were living in were extremely difficult. Such violence toward one another was becoming the norm.

"You will *not* be traveling by speedboat," Mateo said, taking a long draw on his cigarette.

"Listen," Edi said. "You'll be leaving from Durrës." He smiled nervously, beads of perspiration standing out on his forehead. "On the ferry. You'll arrive in Bari, Italy. Besim, an Albanian guy, will be waiting for you. No speedboat, I promise. Here, look." Edi removed the tickets from his shirt pocket and showed them to Dad.

Deti and I sat like wooden dolls, feeling numb and praying that this wasn't going to take a turn for the worst. Our fate hung in the balance as Dad took his time to consider the pros and cons of the new proposed method of travel. Mom stroked my head while Uncle Berti ruminated, all of us almost certain Dad would refuse the plan and insist we go home.

"Okay," Dad said, nodding.

Mom let out a sigh of relief.

The ferry didn't sound as exciting or straightforward as the plane, but it didn't matter as long as it all worked out.

"I'll drive you to Durrës," Uncle Berti said, his face still flushed with anger. "I want to see for myself that you get on the ferry."

Mateo handed Dad a few pieces of paper and an envelope. "Here are the instructions, the tickets, Besim's phone number, and a thousand dollars in lire for him. He'll help you go to France."

Edi and Mateo got into their black car, and we followed them to the seaport of Durrës, arriving in the late afternoon.

"All right, this is it," Uncle Berti said in a gruff voice. His eyes were red and rimmed with tears he was struggling to hold back. Silently he unloaded our things, got back into his car, and, without hugging us or saying a proper goodbye, drove away. Only once did he look back.

Suddenly, it felt as if I were sitting in a theater and watching my life play out on the screen. Something new and strange was happening. Everything was changing. We were the main characters in this new drama, but the script was still missing. Deti and I glanced over at Mom and Dad. We were hurting inside—a deep ache. What was it? A longing, an emptiness?

I couldn't identify the source of the sorrow. Here we were, all alone, just the four of us, standing at the port with our suitcases as large black clouds rolled over, covering up the last traces of the sun, and it started to rain. Rain and tears, tears and rain—who could tell the difference?

Our neighbor Mrs. Braka used to say, "It is not good to cry before a journey. It brings bad luck." Her words echoed in my mind as we wiped away our tears. It was Saturday, July 24, 1999, a date I would always remember.

Today, we were leaving Albania.

CHAPTER 11

Flight from Albania

Deti

July 24–25, 1999

A long line of people waited to board the ferry. Everyone looked nervous. As we stood with the others, an officer from the ship shouted to an old man and woman, "There's no more room today. And no more ferries. Come back tomorrow."

The old man shook his head and muttered something under his breath, his face filled with despair. He put his arm around his wife, and the two shuffled away. How could the officer send them away? At that age, they must have had a good reason to leave Albania.

And what about us? I turned to Mateo next to me. "Do we have to wait until tomorrow too?" I was afraid to hear his answer.

"No, there's another ferry leaving in two hours," he said confidently. He nodded his head in the direction of the elderly couple. "Don't worry about them."

How did he know? I started to say something and then stopped, not wanting to cause any trouble. I surely didn't want to make Mateo angry. But what was going on? If another ferry would come in two hours, why did the officer lie to those people? And how did Mateo know he wouldn't tell us the same thing? Mateo seemed too calm, too certain.

I thought highly educated people, like the officer, never lied. At least that was what I'd heard from adults. Maybe the crisis had changed things. Maybe lying had become normal. Yet if it was okay to tell lies, it could be so easy to trust the wrong person.

For two long hours we waited for the next ferry, staring out beyond the sea, out toward infinity, as the rain slowed to a drizzle. We waited and waited, and then finally, a large, hulking shape of a vessel approached. It reminded me of the *Titanic* in the movie starring Leonardo DiCaprio. If someone had told me that the ferry was unsinkable, I would have definitely believed them.

The gray hulk made it look like a whale, moving as if it owned the sea, like there was nothing bigger or better. How sure it was of its power and majesty as it cut through the waves. It was so large, my anxiety melted away and I smiled excitedly.

This was the first time I'd ever seen a ferry up close, and as luck would have it, we were at the front of the line. I couldn't help stretching out my hand as far as it would reach, wanting to touch this beautiful ferry. Even if the journey wasn't successful, even if it never happened, I could tell my friends what a ferry looked and felt like.

I was almost two meters away from it, still too far away to touch. I moved closer. Just then, Gita yanked at my jacket, a stern reminder that I needed to contain my excitement.

My face grew hot. I must have caught everyone's eyes with my silly behavior. Gita was my tutor, reminding me I had to act like an adult—especially now that the boarding officer had appeared, a tall, crusty man with mean eyes.

He studied our visas and took his time studying each of us. A half laugh, half sneer escaped from the side of his mouth.

"And where, sir, do you think you are going with these visas?" He squinted at Dad. "Your wife's business visa includes your children? Do you expect me to believe they are part of her business? Do they go with her to all her meetings?"

A shudder passed through me. Suddenly our plan seemed so absurd. A businesswoman wouldn't take her children along on a business trip! Our plan to emigrate was too transparent. We were supposed to be dealing with an experienced Albanian group who knew what they were doing.

Dad did his best to stay calm, smiling angelically at the officer. "I understand your concerns, but we're traveling on legitimate business."

"Like hell you are. There's no way I'm going to let you on." The officer swept his arm over us. "Step aside, please. Let these other people by. Next!"

Dad steered us away from the entrance to the ferry. A short distance from us, Mateo had been watching. Without Dad saying a word to him, he went over to the officer. "What's the matter?" he asked.

I couldn't hear what they were saying, but I could see what was going on. Mateo reached into his black trousers, pulled out a wad of money, and quickly placed it in the officer's waiting hand. Deftly, the man palmed it and safely lodged it in his white trousers. Black to white, Mateo to the officer.

I felt weak, almost faint. So this was how it was done. This was much different than Andon, our milkman, watering down our milk. This was the real outside world. Harsh and dirty. The real world of cops and robbers, where money was more than just currency. It greased the wheels of fortune and determined each person's destiny.

The officer was now more than happy to help us escape. "Come on ahead with your family, sir," he shouted, glaring at Dad. "But I can guarantee that you won't make it through the hands of the Italian authorities. You'll be on the next ferry back to Albania."

Though Dad showed no reaction, I knew he was just as worried as the rest of us. He put his arm around my shoulders and gave me a quick hug. "We'll all be fine."

I clutched the Holy Virgin Mary figurine. She would protect us.

By this time, it was dark, but there were no stars. It was still overcast. The sky must have been grieving for our departure. We boarded the ferry and found four seats together on the left side of the deck. Out the windows, all we could see was black ocean.

The ferry heaved and rolled from side to side, buffeting the waves, rocking up and down and back and forth. Feeling dizzy, I grabbed Gita's hand, clammy with nerves. After all that we had lived through, we couldn't easily cast aside our fears. What if something bad happened? What if the ship sank like the *Titanic*? How would we survive?"

If we did go down, I'd have to save Gita because she couldn't swim. But she was supposed to stay strong and be *my* protector.

Gita must have been thinking the same thing. She turned to me, and as our eyes met, she smiled softly. I squeezed her hand as if to reassure her, to reassure myself. Together we were stronger.

"Is there something wrong with the ferry?" I asked Dad. "Is it supposed to go up and down so much?"

"No, this is normal. We'll be there soon."

"How soon is 'soon'?"

Dad didn't answer.

As the ferry moved, I felt worse and worse. Gita too. Holding our stomachs, we tugged at Mom's arm. She looked at me and then at Gita.

Mom pointed to the restroom. "It's over there. I'll come with you."

Gita and I reached the toilets just in time and vomited until there was nothing left. The smell! The awful stuff that came out.

So the ferry wasn't a lot of fun after all. But never mind. My stomach felt much better. Back in our seats, we leaned into each other and soon fell asleep.

Near eight o'clock the next morning, the ferry's horn let out a loud blast, jolting me awake. I had forgotten where I was, but reality quickly set in. We must have arrived at Bari. A strong wind whipped through my hair, thrusting it over my eyes. When I shook my hair away, I couldn't believe the crowds I saw swarming around us.

They pushed and shoved one another as they raced toward the exit, determined to be among the first to get off the ferry. There were so many people, so much noise and chaos, I was afraid we'd all be crushed.

And then came an all-too-familiar BANG!

Gita and I jumped at the same time. What was that? Gunshots?

I clung to her, goosebumps rising on my skin. The past became the present. I was back in Albania, back in the courtyard, the armed man standing so close.

We held on to Mom and Dad and stepped off the ferry into the crowds and confusion. Eventually, we came to three lines. Dad pointed to the one on the right. "I'm going over there. I think it's good if they don't see us together. They might get ideas."

Mom nodded. We stood on either side of her. She was on a business trip and we were on her visa, I reminded myself.

Dad's turn in line came faster than ours. As he handed his papers to the Italian officials, I closed my eyes and begged God to help my father pass through.

Yes! Dad's passport and visa were in order, and the authorities let him through immediately. He smiled and waved at us from the other side.

But it wasn't over yet.

We were waiting behind a pretty brown-haired woman in a black dress and red shoes, carrying a matching red bag. Her makeup was perfect, her red lipstick the finishing touch. She must have been planning to go somewhere special. The officer examined her papers carefully.

The woman kept glancing over her shoulder at us and fussing with her hair. She was having a hard time hiding her nervousness, stammering when the officer talked to her.

He jotted down some notes, gathered the woman's papers, and handed them back to her. "I can't let you go through," he said curtly. "You have a false visa."

She didn't appear shocked by his rejection, but she wasn't ready to accept it, pleading with the officer in Albanian. When she realized he didn't understand what she was saying, she started over again in broken Italian, «*Io passare, passare, incontrare il fidanzato*» (I to pass, to pass, to meet the fiancé).

The officer remained adamant, but when she finally broke down and started to weep, he became sympathetic. "Get this woman a hand-

kerchief," he called over to one of the other men, who came back with
a handkerchief and a glass of water for her.

"You'd better get in line to get a return ticket to Albania," the officer told her. The ferry will depart in an hour."

Our turn now. I held my breath. Would the same thing happen
to us?

Gita whispered to me, "Don't worry. We'll convince them."

My heart was racing. More than anything, I needed to be a good
actress. We didn't take drama classes at school, but surely, I'd learned
something from all the movies we had watched. At that moment, I
had to play the daughter of a man and businesswoman—and I had to
stay calm.

Mom handed all our documents to the officer. I studied him to
see what kind of person he was. Large green eyes, bushy black eyebrows, and thick hair combed back in a fashionable style. No doubt,
his appearance was important to him, but all I could see was how
formidable he looked. The man held our fate in his hands.

Mr. Handsome inspected everything, and then he picked up a pen
from the table and wrote some notes on a yellow pad. We stood on
our tiptoes and craned our necks to see what he was writing, but all
we could see was a big letter "X" written at the end of his notes. Did
that mean we couldn't pass?

It couldn't. No.

"Thank you, madam," he said. "Please go to the room on your
left and take a seat."

Confused, Gita and I followed Mom into the small gray room,
and we sat on one of the old, badly scratched benches. A noisy black
clock hung on the wall across from us. This didn't seem right. It felt
like we were being punished.

"What will they do to us?" I asked Mom.

My Albanian friends told me that in Greece the authorities beat
refugees with whips and put them in jail before sending them back
to Albania. What if the Italian officers beat us? They would probably
beat Dad too.

Mom whispered, "They may make us return to Albania. Please, God, help us." She bowed her head, praying silently.

I clasped the Virgin Mary statue tightly, feeling more secure. I had to get her attention. Only she could help us.

Opposite the prison-like room, Dad leaned against the wall waiting, his black suitcase by his feet. He kept glancing at his watch. The officer from the ferry stood next to him. Why was that obnoxious man there? He was probably feeling triumphant, eager to tell Dad, "See? I told you that you wouldn't make it to Italy."

I went to the door and shouted, "Dad!"

He waved, his smile wary now.

Sometimes dreams that seem impossible do come true. Even mountains that seem too steep and insurmountable can be climbed.

I had heard it before. Everyone tells you it's all over. You're like a wounded bird—your wings drop and you feel drained of energy and hope. But then suddenly, slowly, you recover your strength and start to fight. Gradually another part of you awakens, giving birth to belief, to the conviction that you *can* do it. You can climb that mountain and overcome all odds.

This powerful feeling is stronger than any physical, mental, or emotional aspect of yourself. It is your instinct, your will. And when it speaks, your whole world listens. On that chilly night, everything seemed impossible. We couldn't pass the borders into Italy. Yet my instincts, my will, told me that we'd make it.

Dad must have felt the same strength, the same instinct, because he refused to purchase the return tickets to Albania, despite what the ferry officer had said.

In that gray-walled cell of a room, the noisy clock reminded me that time was passing and we still had no news. Gita was biting her nails while Mom, so sad, so pensive, stared at the clock. I took her hand, and she jumped. I rolled the gold band off her ring finger and kissed it, giving it the fullness of my love. Then I gently put it back on her finger. My love would protect Mom from any negative decisions the tough-looking officer might reach.

Finally, after almost an hour and a half, Mr. Handsome called outside the door, «*La famiglia Zalli*?» We followed him to the passport control area where two other officers were waiting.

"A businesswoman with two kids on your visa?" Mr. Handsome said. "Sorry, madam, but your family can't pass the Italian borders. The ferry to Albania will be leaving in half an hour."

"So we'll have to book return tickets after all," Mom murmured to us in a resigned manner.

On the right, Dad was approaching us. Not far from him, I could see the Albanian ferry officer smirking. A bad sign.

"I'm sorry, but there's really nothing we can do," Dad said wearily. "We're going back. I'm coming with you."

Mr. Handsome stood next to him, nodding as if he understood what we were saying in Albanian.

I looked first at Mom and then at Dad, both hanging their heads in defeat. The Italian officers had just ended our dream, and Mom and Dad were simply accepting what they were told.

No! We couldn't go back without a fight. The heat rushed to my face, and my stomach churned with anger. I reached for Gita. She was close to tears. I couldn't rely on her—it was up to me. I thought of my idol, the Italian soccer star Alessandro Del Piero. He could easily dribble past four or five players on the field anytime he wanted to. I needed to try dribbling too. I had nothing to lose.

I inhaled deeply so I could take in enough air to push out my courage. This was my only chance. I took another deep breath and prepared to fight, clutching Saint Mary in my right hand.

A third deep breath. My tone had to be authoritative, confident. I had to convince them. And then I heard the beautiful Italian words rolling off my tongue, «*Che dice, signore? Questo passaporto è valido, così come il visto. Se dubiti della loro autenticità, dovresti verificarlo sul tuo computer*» (What are you saying, sir? This passport is valid, and so is the visa. If you doubt their authenticity, you should check it on your computer).

Mr. Handsome stared at me, his mouth wide open. The other officers looked our way. I had no clue where this was going to take me. What did I know about how a computer worked? It was a dribble on the field—a gambler's bluff. I hoped and prayed they would buy my lie.

The officers paused. Gita's hand tightened around mine. A signal. We were now two on the soccer field. Del Piero wasn't alone. I passed the ball to Gita. She ran fiercely.

«*Per favore, signori, dateci l'opportunità del dubbio e verificate i nostro documenti*» (Please, gentlemen, give us the benefit of the doubt and verify our documents).

We had attracted the attention of not one but three immigration officers. They exchanged glances. It was hard to tell whether they were surprised by our excellent Italian or simply taken aback because we were only thirteen. Clearly, we had taken up the fight for our parents.

We didn't give them time to reply. We insisted, informing them indignantly, that we knew what we were doing. They had no right to tell us our passports and visas weren't valid.

It was working! We were deep in the game, forgetting all else except the ball. We were making these men think. They started to deliberate among themselves.

My legs were shaking as I waved my arms and continued to speak loud and fast in perfect Italian to the officers. Two of them looked like they might relent. But it wasn't over yet. There was one more we had to get past so we could score—the green-eyed goalkeeper, Mr. Handsome.

We ran toward the goalpost without stopping. Gita and I hit the ball with everything we had.

Mr. Handsome held up his hands in protest. «*Basta! Calmatevi bambine! Io sono buono*» (Enough! Calm down, girls! I am a good person).

He had a word with the two officers, who told him, «*Lasciali andare!*» (Let them go!)

But the goalkeeper was as stubborn as a donkey. Again, we started up, running, running, running. Now it was Del Piero and Gita against the goalkeeper. We could do it. We had a chance.

Oh the words that flowed from our mouths!

The goalkeeper seemed nervous. He struggled to keep his position, to defend the post. «*Questo visto d'affari non è credibile, e sia io che voi lo sappiamo*» (This business visa is not credible, and you and I know it), he snapped to the other two officers, shaking his head. «*Non ci credo per niente. Ma questa volta, chiuderò un occhio*» (I don't believe it for a minute. But this time, I will turn a blind eye).

Gita and I scored! Did we win? Careful. I had to keep my feet on the ground. I had to be serious. It wasn't over yet. I tightened my grip on Gita's hand. Respectfully, like two adults, we hid our joy in front of the officers. It was so hard to keep acting when we had won the game.

«*Grazie mille, signore, non ti dimenticheremo mai*» (Thanks ever so much, sir. We shall never forget you), I said to the goalkeeper with a small, polite smile on my face. After all, he did just give me the opportunity to score.

«*Ora vai, prima che cambi idea*» (Now go, before I change my mind), Mr. Handsome growled.

Mom and Dad had been standing to one side, watching our performance, awestruck. We had forgotten all about them. They must not have realized that we spoke such fluent Italian.

I even surprised myself and Gita too. It felt as though someone had helped us pronounce those words. Someone had helped us rev up our determination and transmit our hearts' desire into their hearts. That someone was in the palm of my hand. *Thank you, Mother Mary.*

Tonight, she taught me if you really wanted something, you could get it, because deep inside, you knew the steps you needed to take to succeed.

How could I describe what I felt? Gita and I had reached the top of the world and touched the sky with our little fingers. A triumphant moment. We had won a difficult international game. Albania against Italy, and we scored in the final half. Just the two of us. We had our destiny in our hands. Once again, we believed in ourselves. We would make it to England.

Outside the check-in area, it was raining hard and the temperature had dropped. I shivered from the cold, but I didn't care. Not even the chilly air and torrential downpour could dampen my spirits. I skipped and splashed in the puddles while Dad bought a telephone card so he could talk to Besim, our contact in Italy, to let him know we had made it into the country.

Dad took a long, deep breath and blew it out, as if releasing all his fears. He joined my dance in the rain. Time to celebrate!

CHAPTER 12

Ciao, Italia

Deti

July 25–27, 1999

At last, a robust young man of medium height with dark hair approached us. "You're the Zalli family, right?" he asked.

"Yes! You must be Besim." Dad stepped forward and shook his hand.

"I apologize for taking so long. In fact, I was on time and waited for you, but then Mateo called and said you didn't make it, so I headed back to Foggia. When you called me, I was halfway there. I turned around immediately, but with the heavy traffic and the rain, the road isn't easy. It makes everything worse."

"Please don't worry about us waiting. We didn't know we were going to pass the borders either." Dad smiled broadly. "Let me introduce you to my wife, Dita, and my daughters, Argita and Detina."

We all set out behind him. It was pouring so hard we could barely see where we were going. When we reached his small car, Besim opened the back doors. "Please make yourselves comfortable."

The car wasn't empty. A young man, apparently a friend of Besim's, sat in the front. In the back, Gita and I squeezed in between Mom and Dad. Somehow we all managed to fit, our suitcases snugly packed into the trunk. I felt protected and warm.

Besim turned the key in the ignition, and the engine coughed and groaned, then started to come alive. The car crept forward. I didn't blame it for balking. It was pulling six people and four large suitcases.

Besim lit up a cigarette and looked at Dad through the rear-view mirror. "How did they let you through? They would have been justified, legally, to turn you back. What made them change their minds?"

"My daughters convinced them," Dad said proudly.

"Really! How?"

The adults carried on an animated conversation as the car labored toward Foggia and I drifted off to sleep. The next thing I knew, Mom was touching my shoulder. "Wake up, sweeties. We've arrived."

I opened my eyes. We were parked in front of what appeared to be a modern Italian home. Standing at the door was a young brunette, about twenty years old, holding a beautiful baby girl.

"Hi, I'm Valbona, Besim's wife, and this is our daughter, Keisi. It is so nice to meet you. Come in!"

We followed Valbona through a narrow corridor, Gita ahead of me. My stomach rumbled loudly. I tapped on Gita's shoulder but she ignored me. I pulled her hair.

"What now?" she asked impatiently.

"I'm starving," I whispered in her ear.

"Wait until tomorrow morning."

"*Tomorrow?*"

Gita followed all of Mom's rules. And Mom taught us to be polite and never ask for food or anything else that might make us a nuisance to others. Our behavior was a reflection on her, she said, which gave us all the more reason to mind our manners.

I had to be a model child, like Gita. Biting my index finger, I convinced myself that sleep was what I really craved. Valbona showed us around the house. It wasn't as beautiful as it looked from the outside. The kitchen had some old broken bricks, and the sitting room had nothing but a tiny couch. There was only one bedroom. Where were we going to sleep?

Besim placed an air mattress on the floor of the sitting room and apologized, saying that was the best he could do for us. We snuggled up together, too cold and tired to care.

I closed my eyes and pushed the hunger from my mind. The sooner I went to sleep, the better. My body sank into the mattress, releasing all the fear and anxiety of the past week. All gone.

In the morning, Valbona called us to breakfast. By then, I was famished. We sat around the table and ate something called brioche and drank Italian milk. It was better than what we could get at Andon's in Albania.

"So, how can I tell you two apart"? Valbona asked.

"I have a mole on my right cheek," I said.

"Ahh, I see." She smiled.

I liked the way she talked. Soft-spoken. There was something riveting about her, and I hung on every word.

She was a refugee, just like we were going to be soon. But I had imagined it all wrong—her life was far from luxurious. She didn't have a washer and dryer. She didn't even have a place to hang out her family's clothes to dry, other than over the railing of the balcony. So this was another part of being a refugee.

After breakfast, Besim and Dad talked about the rest of our journey. "We need to leave very early in the morning," Besim said. "We'll catch the train for Milan, and from Milan, you'll continue on without me to Paris, where another guide will give you further instructions."

That meant we would have to go through at least two different passport control points. How would our luck hold up? We couldn't hope to get lucky again. For sure, we would get caught. I just knew it. How could we avoid it?

To distract us, Besim took us out for a walk around Foggia. The town was known as the granary of Italy, he said, and despite its small size, it was one of the most important towns for the agriculture industry.

The town was clean and orderly, with impressive historical monuments, museums, and churches. I focused hard on all the details so I could describe Foggia to my friends. Who knew how our journey would end. This could be my one and only visit to Italy during my entire lifetime. Next week, I might find myself in Albania again.

In the afternoon we returned, tired and hungry, to Besim's house, and Valbona served us a huge dinner. The wooden table was laden with pasta, pizza, salad, turkey, and three different kinds of cheeses I had never seen before, along with panettone, a light yellowish bread with raisins and lemon zest.

We had never tasted such wonderful food. After eating as much as we could and talking and laughing with our new friends, all four of us squeezed together on the air mattress. Sleep came fast.

I was dreaming of noisy trains when Mom tapped my shoulder. "Kids, it's time to get up. We need to leave for the train station. Besim is waiting in the car. Put on your clothes and shoes. Quick, get a move on!"

I groaned. It was three-thirty.

How could Mom be wide awake? Getting up early was one of the things Gita and I hated the most, and on that particular morning, I would have paid anything just to sleep a little longer.

After rubbing my sleepy eyes, I saw Valbona standing tall beside the sitting room door, ready to say goodbye to us. Her pink dressing gown was rumpled, and she yawned as she leaned back and looked into her bedroom to check on Keisi. How nice of her to get up so early to see us off.

"You'll be okay, girls, don't you worry," she said softly, giving us a big hug.

I hugged her back. I was sorry to leave her. Would I ever see her again? Mom and Dad told us that Besim and Valbona had been refugees for many years. They understood our plight better than anyone.

CHAPTER 13

Milan

Gita

July 27, 1999

We piled into the car and took off into the night. Not far down the road, Dad turned to Besim from the passenger seat. "Mateo told me to give you a thousand dollars in lire."

"That's correct," Besim said.

"Then I better give it to you before we leave your car. We don't want anybody to see us with that amount of cash." Dad pulled out his wallet.

Besim stuffed the money into the pocket of his jeans. Now, I got it. His true income came from working with the doctor, Edi, and Mateo, helping Albanians escape under the radar. My perception of these people had changed. A week ago, I would have described them all as corrupt, but not anymore.

So many things had happened over the past forty-eight hours. My feelings were tangled up in knots. Guilt intertwined with innocence. Worry with calm. I had feelings I couldn't name. But I believed that every human being had a right to live in peace. If our native country had become lawless, then surely, nothing was "wrong" or "corrupt" about us seeking refuge or citizenship in another country.

At least we deserved the right to try.

Like Besim and Valbona, who were trying hard to survive in Italy. Despite being considered "illegal aliens," Besim still hoped he would get Italian documents and Keisi would have a bright future. But Besim said that refugees had to endure plenty of sacrifices and obstacles just to be safe and to have a chance for a decent life.

It was still dark when we arrived at the train station, and even though it was summer, a cold wind whistled around the corners of the station, whipping at our clothes. We grabbed our suitcases and hurried to the platform. It was deserted. No wonder, most people were still asleep at that hour.

I fantasized that my parents were rich businesspeople, with indefinite regular visas, and we were on holiday. We were standing there confidently, like ordinary travelers, waiting for a train to Milan where we would be vacationing. Maybe Dad would do some business while—

"Dad, when is the train coming?" Deti interrupted my reverie.

"Soon, I'm sure," he said.

It was impossible to see anything in the dark. I peered down the tracks for a glimpse of light and listened for the sound of an approaching train. Nothing.

A few minutes later, Deti pointed toward the tunnel, and we could see a yellow beam of light piercing the darkness. The beam grew larger and larger. A train! I let out a laugh. Deti's eyes were shining. Soon we would be on our way to Milan.

This would be our second train ride. Our first was ten years before, in 1989, when we were only three years old. That was when Albanian trains traveled no faster than ten to twenty kilometers per hour. The passenger cars used to be almost luxurious, with coaches that had tables for eating, but over time, they were neglected and became shabby. Even so, it was a fun ride. The waitresses gave each of us a pink-and-white peppermint stick.

This train to Milan was altogether different. The interior was modern and spacious. We settled into our comfortable seats, and I pressed my nose against the window, eager to take in all the scenery. But after the train accelerated, I got dizzy watching everything speed by in a blur.

The train had two small bars where people could sit and eat. The only passengers besides the four of us and Besim were half a dozen young men, all of them laughing and joking around. For a moment they made me forget that we weren't in Italy on a holiday.

Maybe, one day, we, too, would be ordinary passengers. But then the fear monster appeared, pulling me back to reality. I couldn't get rid of him, the beast who always lurked in the shadows, reminding me that something bad would happen if anyone found us out. We had to be so careful and as inconspicuous as possible. We must never be caught.

At dinner the night before, Valbona explained that in other people's eyes, refugees were often pushed to the bottom of the social ladder. In a world where everyone valued their possessions, social standing, and money, a person who had none of those things was looked down upon. I clasped the Mother Mary figurine. I wasn't alone. She would help us, no matter what.

The train slowed, and I looked at my watch. Noon. After eight long hours, we had finally arrived in Milan. Deti smiled and held my hand as we stepped off the train and looked around. The station was so grand. We had entered another world! Wide-eyed, Deti and I pointed at the beautiful architecture, the marble floor, the enormous glass canopy above us. It took my breath away.

But Besim's eyes were fixed on the police around the station and the throngs of people. He motioned for us to come closer. "Girls, please pretend not to be so impressed and excited. If you really were a rich family and your parents were businesspeople, the police would expect you to have traveled abroad before."

Of course. He was right.

"Where are we going now, Mr. Besim?" Deti asked.

"We'll have to wait here for your train to Paris."

"And when does it leave exactly?"

Besim looked at his watch. "At 1:45. An hour and a half."

There was a lot to see and do here and so little time to take it all in. Whether I was an illegal alien or not, I vowed to make the best of it, to see as much as I could and enjoy every single minute. As long as we acted like rich, unimpressed girls, we wouldn't attract any attention.

"Mr. Besim, where should we wait?" Deti asked.

I jabbed her with my elbow. "Stop being a nuisance, will you?"

"He doesn't mind me asking questions. "Isn't that true, Mr. Besim?"

He didn't answer. I turned back to him, but I couldn't see him. "Where did he go?"

Mom and Dad looked all around us and shook their heads.

So strange. He simply vanished. And my excitement went with him. What if he was really gone? What if he wasn't the nice guy he seemed to be? How on earth would we get by in this foreign city without him?

I tugged at Dad's sleeve. "Would he just leave us here?"

"Shhh," Dad whispered. "The police are checking people's documents. See them over there?" He nodded to his right.

Yes, they were there, stopping everyone.

"Mr. Besim has no papers, Gita. You knew that, didn't you?"

"But he was supposed to stay with us, wasn't he? Isn't that what he got paid for, to look out for us?" The familiar panic rose to my throat. How could he abandon us? He was a coward and a deserter. Who was going to explain our situation to the police? "Dad, if the police check on us, we're ruined, right?"

"Will you stop asking so many questions!"

He was just as angry and scared as the rest of us. We squeezed together on a bench and watched the policemen work their way through the crowd. Every second passed in torture.

It was too late for us to disappear. What would they do to us? Lock us up in a prison? Beat us?

"Don't look frightened," Dad said to the three of us, his voice stern. "We must all appear calm and relaxed or they'll suspect something is wrong."

Quickly, I ran a hand over my face to remove any signs of fear. This was a repeat of what happened with the Italian border officers.

I stared at Deti and forced her to meet my eyes. "Come with me. It's time to play."

She understood. Right now, our performance was everything. We were the daughters of wealthy businesspeople. Rich girls. Like the bored children of wealthy parents, we had to find a way to amuse ourselves.

Deti jumped to her feet and put on her Joan of Arc mask, Deti the Fearless Warrior. She played her role so well she nearly convinced me that she wasn't scared anymore. I took off in a run. "Let's race!" I yelled.

She chased after me. I glanced over my shoulder, pretending to check on her, to see how far away she was, but I was really looking for the police. Where were they? Out of the corner of my eye, I saw them moving close to Mom and Dad.

"Can't catch me!" I yelled.

I changed directions and ran toward Mom and Dad, passing through the policemen, as if I could miraculously divert them from going closer to them. Out of breath, Deti came up behind me, and we sat on either side of Mom and Dad to protect them. But what could we do?

The policemen were just a few steps away. There was nothing we could make up in Italian that would work this time. My heart was thumping so loud. The game was over. They would send us back to Albania.

I gripped the pendant Frida had given me. She said everything would be okay and so did Auntie Ani. I closed my eyes so I couldn't see the police as they approached us. If I couldn't see them, I wouldn't be as frightened.

As their footsteps got louder, I steeled myself for the worst. But then they seemed softer and more distant. I didn't hear their voices. Cautiously I peered through my fingers to get a glimpse, pretending to rub my eyes, and I couldn't believe what I was seeing.

No one was in front of us. Where were they? I opened my eyes wide and searched the crowds, the train platform, and the yard beyond. No uniforms anywhere. I looked at Dad, waiting for confirmation. Grinning, he gave me a thumbs-up.

A miracle!

What happened? Somehow we escaped again. But just barely. I could breathe again, the heavy weight lifted from my shoulders. I jumped up from the bench and took off in another run, Deti close behind.

We lined up together at a starting point and raced each other to the end of the train yard and back as if nothing had happened. We were becoming experts at deception. And now that the police were gone, we had a whole hour left to enjoy ourselves.

When we rejoined Mom and Dad, they were laughing, a sound more beautiful than anything in the world. We would be okay. Everything would work out according to plan.

Suddenly, as if he agreed with me, Besim appeared, navigating through the crowd of people. He still walked with caution, casting uneasy glances, trying to spot the police, but he moved steadily toward us.

Deti saw him too. "Look, Mom! There's Besim!"

"Yes, I see him. We were expecting him. He wouldn't have run away, of course. Don't forget, he has a young wife and a little baby in Foggia waiting for him to come back. He has to think about them too."

Dad went over to meet Besim, and the two walked outside, Besim all smiles now, with the attitude of someone who did nothing wrong. But thinking about what Mom just said, I understood. I had no right to blame him.

Out in the vast square in front of the train station, the sun hit my face. Summers in Milan must be beautiful. It was hot, like it was Albania, so we were used to it. But I wasn't used to all the pigeons. I'd never seen so many. They hardly left us a place to walk. Oh how they fought for a piece of bread!

At the far end of the square, Deti called out, "Gita, are you coming or what? C'mon! I'm waiting for you."

I dashed off in her direction. When she swiftly darted to the right,

I followed her lead. But then she suddenly stopped as she sensed I would catch her.

Back in Albania, Deti had been the leader of the neighborhood kids. She would quit if she thought she might lose because that would go against her reputation—the heroine never lost. When it came to games, my twin was as cunning as a fox and as clever as a crow.

"That wasn't cool," I said, coming up to her. "You tricked me. I would have won."

Deti placed her hand on my neck, wrapping her fingers around the softer part where I'm ticklish. "Would you really have won?" she teased.

I lowered my head and laughed, no longer able to speak. "Nooo, not at all!" I managed to say.

Deti slid her hand away. "Good," she said with a smirk.

She laid an arm on my shoulder, our sign of peace. No hard feelings. As we rested, I glanced across the square and saw a tall man with a chubby-looking boy coming toward us. The man looked like Uncle Dalan, Mom's younger brother. He had immigrated to Milan nine years before. And the boy looked like Cousin Andi, Uncle Nori's son, who lived with Grandma Lako in Albania. He had come to spend the summer holidays with Uncle Dalan.

My stomach flipped with excitement. Could it really be them? What were the chances? I stared at the two, rubbing my eyes to make sure they weren't deceiving me.

"Deti, see that man and boy over there?" I pointed at them. "Don't they look like Uncle Dalan and Cousin Andi?"

She studied the pair. "You're right. They look a lot like them." She held her hand above her eyes to block the sun. "It *is* Uncle Dalan!"

"It can't be." I shook my head. "That's too much of a coincidence— what would he be doing here?"

"I guarantee you it's them."

"Mom!" We both shouted as we ran toward her, interrupting her conversation with Dad and Besim. We weren't very polite about it, but surely they wouldn't mind.

Mom only had to look at the man for a second. "Yes, it's Dalan! How is that even possible?" She smiled broadly, her face lighting up, her beautiful green eyes sparkling.

Mom and Uncle Dalan had been inseparable when they were growing up, and she missed him terribly since he immigrated to Italy. With such poor phone services in Albania, she couldn't talk with him much. As the youngest of Grandma Lako's ten children, only one year apart, they were as close as Deti and me. The family's poverty brought them even closer together. When Mom was ten years old and Lako and Baba were working, Mom would cook for Dalan and check his homework every evening.

And when it was cold and the electricity was cut off throughout Patos, Mom and Dalan would dig a big hole and put their feet inside it to warm each other up. She was a protective older sister, often saving him from the pranks Uncle Berti would play on him.

Today, Dalan was a different person. The tall young man's fitted blue trousers and red shirt made him look Milanese. He had turned his world around. Poverty had been only a temporary phase for him.

"Dalan! Dalan!" Mom shouted.

Uncle Dalan stopped and searched through the crowd to see who was calling him. When he saw Mom, his eyes grew curious, and as Mom called out to him again, they widened in surprise. He ran toward us, little Andi following him.

I looked up at the sky and smiled. Was luck playing with us today, or was it being truly generous? I could hardly move as the two approached each other. It was like a movie.

Uncle Dalan opened his arms and Mom fell into them. Then it was our turn. He hugged us tightly, taking turns kissing each of us again and again. Puffing furiously, Andi reached us and joined our hugging circle. We hadn't seen him for over two months. It was the longest we'd ever been apart.

What a reunion—and this time in Milan! The Mother Mary figurine that Auntie Ani had given us had secretly hidden this magnificent gift. I felt so blessed. Uncle Dalan took us to one of his favorite restaurants near the train station. It was like a palace, the tables covered with white tablecloths and set with gleaming silverware and vases of fresh-cut flowers.

We sat in the corner by the window, and each of us ordered a huge scoop of chocolate ice cream. It was beyond delicious, like nothing I'd ever tasted before. Now that Uncle was with us, we could relax. He wouldn't abandon us even if the police caught us. Deti, Andi, and I chattered away while the adults caught up on all the news.

Before we knew it, it was 1:30.

"We have to go," Dad said, interrupting our conversation.

At once, like trained soldiers, we pushed back our chairs. For an entire hour, we had forgotten who we were and what we were doing. My eyes filled with tears. When would we see them again?

CHAPTER 14

Ce N'est Pas Juste

Gita

July 27–28, 1999

The trip to Paris would be long, but we were prepared to make the best of it. After boarding the train, we got comfortable in our seats, and for the first hour or so, Deti and I relived every moment of Milan with Uncle Dalan and Andi. We talked happily, yet lying just beneath our excitement was a fear that neither of us wanted to confront. We saw it in the faces of our parents. Sleep was now a luxury for them, one that they couldn't afford. They had to stay alert to protect our luggage and watch everyone around us, especially the officials.

Eventually the motion of the train, the rhythmic clack-clack-clack of the wheels gliding over the tracks, lulled Deti and me into a light sleep. But when the conductor came to check our tickets, I jolted upright, afraid once again. The conductor reminded me too much of a policeman about to check our passports and send us home.

Somehow, the hours passed. I slept fitfully, waking up from time to time to check on Mom and Dad. At midnight, we finally arrived in Paris at Gare Saint Lazare. Bleary-eyed, we stepped off the train and glanced around for our next travel guide, relieved to see no sign of the police.

So far, so good.

Throughout the large, brightly lit station, throngs of people hurried past as one train after another was announced over the loudspeaker. It was all so strange. We didn't hear a word of English, Italian, Albanian, or any other language except French, which we couldn't understand or speak.

Other passengers reunited with their loved ones, rushing to get a cab or waiting for a bus. Everyone had a home to go to. Was that how we looked to anyone observing us? We couldn't raise any suspicion. No one should get a hint of our plan.

So this was Paris. I held tightly to Deti's hand, feeling lost and confused. Our guide didn't show up outside the platform. As we moved into the waiting area, we were jostled by the swarms of people coming and going. What a bleak, depressing place. The thick cigarette smoke made me sick, and I swallowed hard to keep from throwing up.

All the benches were full, so we huddled near the entrance, assaulted by the incessant conversation and deafening announcements blaring from the tiny loudspeakers. If Deti hadn't been holding my hand, I would have gotten swept away by all the pushing and shoving. Dad motioned for us to follow him, and we slowly made our way through the throng and circled the entire waiting area, searching for someone who might catch sight of us and come forward to identify himself.

Several minutes passed. "Dad, are we waiting in the right place?" Deti asked. "Besim said that when we arrived in Paris, there would be someone waiting to take us to a hotel, and—"

"Yes, yes, yes. I don't know. Maybe he hasn't seen us."

We waited fifteen more minutes, but still no one approached us. It was so unsafe for us to be standing there alone.

Dad had kept his cool, but now his eyes darkened with anger. He started muttering to himself, "Where the hell are you?" His fists clenched, he released a string of words I'd never heard him utter before.

We pushed through the crowd again before another large wave of people kept us from circling the waiting room. Dad concentrated all his anger, tension, and frustrations in his right foot, stamping it on the floor impatiently. Stamp-STAMP . . . stamp-STAMP . . . stamp-STAMP.

He grabbed our hands. "Both of you come with me. The man we're supposed to meet knows you're twins. Since you're wearing identical outfits, he should be able to easily spot you two."

Starting at one end of the waiting lounge, we walked the entire length with him, even going as far as the train platform. As every minute passed, we become even more frightened. Another train arrived, depositing more people, mostly young, a lot of them looking more than a little unsavory. Lots of hustling and bustling, many people in a hurry.

Maybe we weren't that alone after all. Could any of those people be running from the French police? I needed to change my thoughts, be more positive. I was in Paris, one of the most beautiful places in the world. I should be appreciating this trip. How could I be so ungrateful? Just ten hours ago, I was in Milan. I met Uncle Dalan and Andi. Then, for the first time in my life, I got on an express train. When would I have had a chance to get on an express train in Albania? Yes, I was luckier than all of my friends. They would do anything just to step on Parisian soil. And I am here!

More minutes passed and still no sign of anyone. No matter how hard I tried, I couldn't stop my negative thoughts. What did it matter whether we were in Paris or New York? This city was just another place filled with fear and uncertainty, where I couldn't do anything except pray that amid all these strangers speaking a strange language, somehow, somewhere "the man" would show up.

Everyone else walked with a purpose. They knew where they were going. Everyone else understood each other. I had never felt so lost and alone in my whole life with my parents beside me.

A young boy in a T-shirt and jeans pushed up next to me, moving in close.

"*Voulez vous de la drogue?*" he asked us boldly.

I stared incredulously at him, the words echoing in my ears. Although I didn't speak French, I could understand the word *drogue*, since it is pronounced the same in Albanian. Tears stung my eyes. I pulled Dad close so I could talk to him easily. "This is crazy. They're selling drugs here!"

"Come with me." He steered us through the crowd toward one of the shops. "We need to buy a phone card. I have the man's number. We'll call him."

Most of the shops were closed, and the ones that were open had no phone cards. A young French woman was watching us. "*Voulez vous appeler quelqu'un?*"

Not understanding, I shrugged and shook my head. The girl shaped her hand like a phone and held it to her ear. "*Téléphone?*"

I nodded. At least I could understand the word *téléphone* if nothing else. "I don't understand French," I said in English. "But, yes, I would like to call someone, please. Can you help us? I need a phone card."

"*Non, je ne parle pas anglais,*" she said in fluent French. "*Vous attendez quelqu'un?*"

"Do you speak English?

She shook her head. "*Désolé, non.*"

"But you understand a little bit, yes?"

Her face turned red. She looked furious as she walked away from us.

"Dad, she doesn't understand English. She got angry when I kept asking her."

"Don't worry, honey." Dad passed his hand over his forehead, a gesture of frustration and uncertainty I knew too well. "I'm sure someone will help us."

The four of us continued to scan the crowds. Even though the waiting room was still packed, the crowd slowly began to change. The room was full of single travelers now, as well as groups of young men. We were the only family in the waiting room. Surely, if the man was here, he would be able to recognize us. I swallowed the lump in my throat.

On the other side of Dad, Deti was wiping away a tear. I frowned at her to stop her from crying, even though a few minutes ago, I was about to burst into tears myself. If Mom and Dad saw either of us upset or crying, it would only make things worse.

We walked along the platform and sifted through the crowds in the waiting area over and over again, but the man was nowhere to be found. Suddenly someone tapped my shoulder and I jumped.

It was the woman I had just spoken to. "Excuse me," she said in perfect English, "I have no phone cards, but I can let you use my mobile for a few minutes. Who do you want to talk to? Which country?"

Why hadn't she owned up to understanding me earlier? I didn't have time to think about it. She was the only person who had offered to help us, and we had to trust her.

"France," I said. "Thank you!"

"Okay, but please don't talk too long. It costs a lot."

"We'll be quick."

I passed the phone to Dad, who smiled and bowed graciously to the woman. "Thank you, thank you very much."

She smiled back. Little did she know that those were the only words he knew in English.

Dad dialed the number. The three of us looked at him hopefully. Surely the man would answer.

"Come on . . . please," Dad muttered as he dialed the number again and again. Still no answer. "One more time," he said. But it went straight to voicemail. He shook his head.

A hollow ache gnawed at my stomach. What else could we do?

"Gita, explain to the woman that I need her phone for just two more minutes," Dad said. "I'll pay for the call. I need to talk to Edi in Albania."

I relayed the message. The French woman stood near us and nodded, her face full of concern. What would we have done without her kindness?

Dad's fingers trembled as he dialed the number. The phone started ringing, ringing . . . still ringing . . . and then finally Edi's voice gruffly answered.

Dad didn't waste a second. "Do you have any idea what kind of hell you've put us through?" He shouted into the phone. "My wife and kids are with me at the Paris train station, and your irresponsible contact person who was supposed to be our bloody guide isn't here! We aren't safe! We've been looking everywhere for him. We even called his number. No answer."

Edi was saying something, but Dad talked over him. "Now you listen to me. If he doesn't show up in the next ten minutes, we'll return to Albania, and I'll spend the rest of my life telling everyone how you swindle people out of their hard-earned money, promising smooth travel options and no visa problems with your immigration schemes. This wasn't the deal. I've had enough of this nonsense."

Whatever Edi was saying now must have been reassuring. By the end of the conversation, Dad had stopped shouting and looked relieved.

"Thank you very much," he said again to the French woman. She must have been trying to piece together what was happening. Dad returned the mobile phone to her and reached into his pocket for ten francs.

Smiling, she pushed Dad's hand away. "*Non, non, merci, merci. Ce n'est pas necessaire!*"

Soon after she left, a short, young man appeared nearby. Only ten minutes before, I had seen him standing not too far behind us. I had even pointed him out to Dad. He glanced at the man. "No, that's not him," he said. "If it were, he would have approached us ages ago."

The young guy moved closer and then stopped. We all looked his way.

"Hello?" Dad said in Albanian.

The man responded in Albanian.

"Yes?" My father lifted his eyebrows. "Is it you?"

"It's me."

Dad's face registered shock, and then his rage boiled up. "Where the hell have you been? Why weren't you answering the phone? Do you have any idea how long we have been waiting here for you?"

The man leaned forward and tightened his fists. "Who the hell do you think you're talking to? Do you know who I am?"

"I couldn't care less who you are!"

What was Dad thinking? Didn't he know how dangerous this man might be? I pulled on his jacket, my skin prickling with fear. Mom moved closer to him and pressed on his hand as if to stop him.

"Please, Dad, please!" Deti cried out. She clutched the Virgin Mary figurine tightly in her hand, tears rolling down her cheeks.

Dad was no match for this guy, but in his current state, he probably wasn't thinking right. We'd heard all sorts of stories about people getting into fights like this and killing each other. Angrily I yanked the suitcases from Dad, deliberately scraping them against the floor to distract him. I tried to choke back a large sob, but I didn't care anymore if anyone saw me crying. I just wanted us to leave.

As Dad and the man glared each other, ready to leap at each other's throats, Mom moved closer to them. "Listen, we're all tired. We've been looking for each other at this train station for hours and now that we have finally found each other, will you both stop? I'd like to leave before the authorities come get us."

The young man stepped back and put up his hands. "Hey, lady, I'm just here to help you guys. You're the ones with the problem." He shrugged, now completely indifferent.

Dad looked at Mom and then at the man. "Our conversation will not end here," he snarled. Turning away from him, Dad took a few deep breaths and finally calmed down enough to see our tears. "Hey, there's no reason to cry. Everything is going to be okay, I promise." He locked his arms around us. "You heard what he said—this man is going to help us. There was just a slight misunderstanding."

Deti and I glanced dubiously at Dad as we hugged him tightly. I hoped he meant what he said. Wordlessly, the mystery man led the way. Mom took Dad's hand, and the two walked behind him, followed by Deti and me. A few minutes later, we exited the terminal and reached the taxi stand.

"We'll go to the hotel now," the man said to Dad. "Only three people in each taxi. You have to take another one with me." The taxi driver made a note of the hotel's address, and we took off.

But what if Dad argued with the guy? I kept twisting my head around to check on the two of them in the taxi behind us. I could see them talking, but that's all. Fifteen tense minutes later, we arrived at the hotel, and Dad climbed out of the taxi, his eyes no longer stormy. The two must have cleared the air.

We followed the man inside to the hotel reception desk. He showed Mom's and Dad's passports to the woman behind the desk and paid for a double room. When we reached our room at the stop of the stairs, the man finally left.

We closed the door, at last alone with Mom and Dad. The room was simply furnished with an antiquated shower and unpainted walls that made it look dirty, but it was the best place ever because for now it meant we were safe.

I didn't ask any questions about the man, choosing not to know. But our business with him wasn't finished. We were to meet him again in the morning at ten. After such a long, stressful night, I fell asleep as soon as my head touched the pillow.

When we came down to the lobby the next day, the man introduced himself as Ben and apologized to Dad for his behavior. He had no choice, he said, because the French police were after him. No wonder he didn't approach us immediately. But what had he done to be in trouble with the police? He didn't offer any more details, and Dad didn't press him.

On the positive side, Ben took us to a small French restaurant and treated us to orange juice, which we drank with super cool red, yellow, and blue curly drinking straws. We had never seen anything like them before.

Leaning forward, Ben kept his voice low. "For the next part of the trip," he said, "you'll take a train to Boulogne, and then from there, a train to your final destination—London."

"You mean a ferry from Boulogne to England and then a train to London?" Dad asked.

Ben nodded.

"Anything else about the journey we should know?" Dad asked.

"Hmm, no, at least nothing I can think of at the moment." Ben looked around the room, avoiding eye contact. "But my advice is to be very careful. You never know how things will go from here. It's not as easy as they say, and I would definitely not bet on a straight-forward journey. Many Albanians have been caught on their way from France to England."

"You know something you're not telling us, don't you?" Dad said, his voice rising. "What did they do? How were they caught?"

"Keep it down. It's nothing. Really. It won't happen to you." Ben waved his hand dismissively.

My mind swirled with questions. What didn't he want us to know about? What else could happen? What more could we possibly have to deal with?

Soon we boarded the train once again, this time heading for the Boulogne-sur-Mer station, a two-and-a-half-hour trip. I sat next to Deti, opposite our parents, not sorry at all that we were leaving Paris.

Over and over, the conversation from the morning replayed in my mind. Sweat trickled down my back as I expected the policemen to appear anytime and send us back home. I tried to hide my uneasiness, but it was bigger than me.

We were about ten minutes outside Boulogne. This leg of the jour-ney was ending soon, and so far, no police. Perhaps we were safe. If policemen were coming, they would have been there by now, unless they were waiting for us on the platform.

But when we stepped off the train, still no police. We left the sta-tion without any problems. It all felt weird. Maybe a little too easy? This part of the trip must not have been what Ben was talking about. Where could the Albanians have been caught?

A beggar distracted me from my deep thoughts. He was lying by the side of the road, covered in grime, an old mug half-filled with pennies the only thing keeping him company. Dirt filled every wrinkle of his old, papery skin. His greasy hair had turned into oily matted strings. His filthy clothes seemed stuck to his body, sucking the life out of him.

All he cared about was the little mug. He rattled it halfheartedly at us and then slumped back against the wall. That was what giving up looked like. Seeing him gave me goosebumps, yet I couldn't tear my eyes away.

"Hi there, is this the Zalli family?"

What a relief. Our guide was walking toward us. He shook Dad's hand and introduced himself. In shorts, probably in his thirties, Naim had a skinny, tanned body and scratches on his arms and legs. He dragged two of our bags along and we followed him to his car, parked at the corner of a narrow road.

He told Dad that he was going to drop us off at the Port de Boulogne-sur-Mer where the rest of the group was waiting for us. The rest of the group? Perhaps they were going+ to advise us on how to get our British papers quickly after we arrived in England. No, that didn't make sense.

"Is it just my family traveling on, or are there other people who will be leaving with us for England tomorrow?" Dad asked.

Naim wrinkled his eyebrows and paused, as if Dad had asked the wrong question.

"Of course, man. There are other people in the queue. They might not depart tomorrow, but they will depart at some point."

"At some point?" Dad asked, taken aback.

"Well, you know how these things go. It really depends on how many trucks we manage to open, and of course, if we don't get caught by the police."

"Trucks?"

"Yes, trucks that carry dog and cat food." Naim laughed. "You know that it's the only way to escape, right?"

CHAPTER 15

No Choice

Gita

July 28–30, 1999

The four of us stared at one another, stunned. A truck carrying dog and cat food?

Dad shook his head. "No, no, I think you must have misunderstood our case. We're going by ferry to England and then by train to London. We're not going in a truck."

I exchanged a helpless glance with Deti, bracing myself for yet another scary situation. This must have been what Ben was trying to warn us about. What Dad would do if we couldn't get on a train? What if he fought with Naim?

"I don't know what you were told, but all these cases are one and the same," Naim said firmly. "We can't take any chances. England is flooding with illegal immigrants, and security has been tightened at all the checkpoints. They've caught thousands of people. You'll be going by ferry, but you'll be in a truck."

Dad grew silent. What would he do? What would he say? Mom patted his back as if to console him. I squeezed Deti's hand so hard it hurt both of us.

Dad's shoulders dropped, as though the weight was too heavy for him to carry anymore. He looked down the street and back at Naim. "All right, truck it is."

What made him agree so quickly? We might never know, but I was relieved to avoid another angry scene.

Mom nodded in agreement. Maybe we'd have better luck this way.

It took us almost a half hour to reach the appointed spot, a huge field called the Den. Other refugees were already there. Many of them had set out their blankets as if they were on a picnic, lying on the damp grass, soaking up the sun.

Like the beggar I left behind at the train station, the men were dirty, with unshaven long beards, unwashed, greasy hair, tattered pants, and shoes splitting at the soles. Some had their eyes closed. I couldn't tell whether they were sleeping or thinking. All of them broken, yet persisting in their fight for that unnameable thing telling them not to give up. They scared me because we had that in common, but I never wanted to be like them.

The silence made me nervous, especially in a bleak spot like this one. An old man with gray hair had covered his face with his cap. Perhaps he wanted to hide from the world or just not exist anymore. He breathed heavily and groaned.

Naim took the lead, and we followed him in a straight line, like ducklings, to a group of four men who would be our guides. Klodi was the one in charge. Tall with black Albanian-Mediterranean features. But his features and height were not the only things that grabbed my attention. His arms and legs were covered with scars and scratches— similar to the ones Naim had.

"There'll be three trucks available tonight," Klodi told us. "At eleven. You might be able to get on one of them."

He prepared us for the journey ahead, explaining that getting into the truck was not going to be as simple as just hopping into the back. Klodi would have to cut the tarp covers, smuggle us inside, and then close them properly to make them appear untouched. The trucks would depart on the 3 a.m. ferry from Boulogne's port and stop at a city in Kent, a county in southeast England.

If all went according to plan, once we arrived in Kent, we would get on the first train to London, where we needed to approach the British authorities and file a report with them. Since the sixteen-month war between the Albanians and Serbs in Kosovo had just ended in June,

Klodi told us to lie about where we were from. If we said we were Kosovars escaping the aftermath of the fighting, it would increase our chances of getting asylum and lower our chances of being deported.

So that was how it worked. I perched quietly on top of our luggage, closed my eyes, and leaned on Deti's shoulder, trying hard to empty my mind and think of nothing.

When I woke up, the air was heavy with resignation. The silence of the other refugees made me think that this was a typical day for them. Maybe they had been there for a while now.

In the late afternoon, Klodi took us to a humanitarian organization called the Red Cross. Inside the huge building was a large hall with unpainted wooden tables and stools. Many French people were there, setting out food for the refugees. Dad said that we shouldn't be shy about eating because everything was free.

Klodi acted as our interpreter. He gave Deti and me an orange chunk of cheese that tasted disgusting, along with some bread. Though the meal wasn't appetizing, we were starving and wolfed it down without complaint. After finishing our meal, we returned to our spot. And waited.

Close to nine-thirty, when it was completely dark, Klodi said that the Boulogne harbor had quieted down. It was time to move.

"All you have to do is follow me and hide if you see the police." He repeated this over and over again, as if it were an easy thing to do. Almost like a mantra. Maybe he wanted to boost our confidence, hoping that we would have success.

It was hard to see in the dark. I stayed close to Klodi, trying to keep up with his pace, and Dad, Mom, and Deti were directly behind me. As we trudged along, Klodi told us to be quiet. We didn't talk or whisper, but sometimes our heavy suitcases made a loud scraping sound as we dragged them across the ground. We could have left them, but they were all we had.

We moved along the narrow street. About a half hour passed. Klodi whispered to me that we were getting closer to the trucks. Thankfully, I didn't see any policemen around.

Suddenly the beam of a flashlight shone ahead of us. Klodi held his arm up, signaling for us to stop. Then he turned and put his finger to his lips, telling us to be quiet, and motioned toward the nearby bushes.

We crouched behind them. The two arcs of light slowly swept over the area, moving closer and closer until we could see the two French policemen holding them.

They stopped about ten meters in front of us. Luckily, the thick bushes provided enough cover to hide us completely so we could watch them unobserved. Two large men, dressed in blue uniforms, each with a whip and a gun.

I put my mouth to Dad's ear. "I'm really scared," I whispered. "What if they kill us? Let's go before it's too late. I want to go home."

He hugged me tightly and whispered back, "Shhh. Everything is going to be okay."

As we watched, Klodi came out of his hiding place and walked up to the policemen. What was he doing? He appeared confident, calm, and, unlike me, unafraid of their whips and guns.

He played his role well, talking to them freely with a warm tone. His voice had laughter in it. He acted as if he were out for a walk and had bumped into two of his best friends, just enjoying a lovely stroll down the road.

It wasn't working. The two policemen kept shaking their heads, not allowing him to pass.

"Come on, Klodi," Dad murmured to himself.

Dad's distress added to my own fears. Where were Mom and Deti? They had been right behind us ten minutes ago. I had lost track of them.

Unable to convince the policemen, Klodi pretended to make his way back to the Den. The policemen watched as he walked down the street. When he came close to the bushes, he signaled to us discreetly to wait a little longer for the police to leave.

I never let go of Dad's hand. After nearly an hour, the police finally left, and the four of us slowly retreated from the bushes and into the darkness, returning to the Den too. We wouldn't reach the dock area on time.

On the night of July 29, 1999, we had no other choice but to camp outside on a park bench that Mom and Dad found nearby in the open area around the Den. We used their knees as our headrests while we sat on the ground, our legs cramping under us. The cold made us shiver, and the wind pierced through our clothes. Our hands and feet were frozen. Mom and Dad covered us with their warm jackets.

I stared into the dark, praying I'd fall asleep and tomorrow would be a better day. As the wind stung my eyes, I looked up and realized the stars were too far away to wish upon.

The next morning, gray storm clouds filled the sky, racing after one another, rolling and swelling. Suddenly, a loud, ear-splitting crack of thunder, and it began to rain, soon giving way to a downpour, drenching everything underneath. Like a heavy cloak, the rain dampened everyone's spirit, suffocating all feelings of hope.

There was no point in trying to escape the weather. We had nowhere to go. Mom's and Dad's jackets were our only shelter, and they offered little protection. We clung to each other, thinking the collective heat from our bodies would keep us warm. Like wild animals, the other travelers had found their own corner and kept their distance. No one was to be trusted.

Only one other family was there, and we quickly made their acquaintance. Eliza and Hiesor were traveling with their three-month-old son. Dad helped them rearrange their luggage to shield the baby from the rain. They smiled and thanked him several times.

Sitting on our luggage, we waited impatiently for the storm to pass and the sky to clear. Even though it was a summer rain, we were chilled to the bone. My teeth wouldn't stop chattering. Maybe the sun would come out and dry everything before we left for the dock again to get on the trucks.

I suddenly remembered the camera I had stashed at the bottom of my suitcase. A friend of Dad's had visited Greece and bought the camera for him as a present. The family put me in charge of using it, and I was so proud to be the one who got to keep it while we traveled. I was supposed to be capturing beautiful scenes, wonderful memories of an amazing trip, the trip of my dreams. I opened the small outer pocket on side of the suitcase and rummaged around until I found the camera.

Watching me, Dad said, "What are you doing, Gita? There's nothing beautiful here."

"Beautiful pictures aren't always of beautiful things." I looked through the camera and tried to get a good angle of the Den. "I'll take a shot of the people here, just as they are. And then I'll use it when I write a book about my life."

"Don't do that." Dad snatched the camera away from me.

"What? Why not?"

"It's not a good idea."

He slipped the camera back into the suitcase pocket. I didn't understand, but I didn't ask and returned to sitting on the luggage.

Slowly, the hours passed. The rain finally stopped, but the sun never came out, and our clothes stayed damp. When it grew dark, Klodi told us to get ready again. He repeated the instructions: follow him and stay quiet. It was easier this time because we knew where we were going and Mom and Dad had figured out how to carry the suitcases without making any noise.

We were almost at the end of the narrow street and about to enter the dock area when a loud voice came from behind us.

"Stop! You must leave this area immediately."

My heart plummeted. We turned around to see the French police. They were speaking English, probably assuming we wouldn't understand French.

"If you come back, we will arrest you. Is that clear?"

We bobbed our heads up and down in unison. Yes, yes, we understood.

As we once again trudged back to the Den, Mom waved her hand from side to side several times. "Gimi . . . this isn't going to work," she said, her voice thick with emotion. It was the first time on this journey that she cried, and it completely broke my resolve to go on.

"Can we go home, Dad?" I said. "I'm scared. I don't want to go to prison. This trip is impossible."

But Deti cried out, "No!" She shook her head, not ready to give up.

"We tried, okay?" Mom said. "I need to call Lefta and let her know we're coming back to Albania."

She walked off. I followed her to a phone booth close to the harbor, and she used the card Dad bought in Boulogne for emergencies. After the weird episode in Paris, he didn't want to travel without one. Now, we could always make calls and not have to rely on the kindness of strangers who might not know English.

"We're coming home, Lefta," Mom said. "Once the water is running again, please fill my plastic bottles."

After all we'd been through, she was worried about the water? I fumed, certain that if I spoke, all the pent-up anger from the trip would explode out of my mouth.

Yet I knew exactly why Mom was thinking like that. We had spent almost three days sleeping outside and we stunk like pigs. At least if we went back, we'd have enough water to take a shower. In Albania, especially in the summer, water shortage was a serious problem.

When we caught up with Dad and Deti, Dad took Mom's hand. "Dita," he said, "let's try one more time. We've come this far and waited this long. I have a feeling it will work out tomorrow." He sounded calm and confident.

"Yes, Mom, please?" Deti said. "They won't catch us, I promise."

Mom took in a big breath and blew it out slowly. She looked at Dad. "Yes, we've come this far, but this is the very last time."

CHAPTER 16

A Third Chance

Deti

July 31, 1999

At midnight, after another long day of waiting, we prepared to go to the truck depot yet again. Klodi told us we had to leave our luggage behind this time.

"It's too risky," he said. "Besides, you and your big suitcases will take up space for six people, not four. Hide the bags somewhere in the bushes, and if you make it to England, I'll mail them to you. If you don't, they'll be waiting for you here. I can assure you that nobody will find them."

Mom sat on the suitcases shaking her head, tears in her eyes. No, she couldn't leave them, she said. Inside were so many treasures, like the gifts her parents gave to her when she married Dad, along with her best clothes and all the precious possessions of a lifetime.

Dad leaned down and put his arm around her. We couldn't hear what he said, but Mom finally stood and let him take the bags. He hid them well. Still, my heart hurt. Would we ever see our things again?

Klodi checked his watch. We needed to hurry. Without the luggage, we moved quickly and quietly, ready to hide behind the bushes if the police showed up again. Klodi signaled all clear, and we successfully passed the first checkpoint where we had been caught before.

We followed Klodi's footsteps, silent as the air, invisible as ghosts. He stopped and signaled all clear again, and we moved forward in the dark. The second checkpoint. We had never gotten that far before.

Lights up ahead. Klodi pointed to the left. A hundred meters away were all kinds of trucks—but they were surrounded by a tall metal fence, and French policemen were everywhere, waiting to lock us up.

We all froze.

What was Klodi thinking? How would we ever get near those trucks?

Klodi waved his hand at the police. "Don't worry, we'll get past them." He tapped Dad's shoulder rapidly. "Gimi, focus. We're going in pairs. It's too dangerous otherwise. Get one of your daughters and follow me. Your wife and other daughter will stay here until I come back for them."

Dad took my hand, and after we both gave Gita and Mom a quick hug, he nodded.

"Okay, let's go," Klodi said.

We walked with slow, silent steps. Dad held my hand firmly, leading the way.

Klodi glanced over his shoulder. "Well done. We're almost there."

As we approached the fence, we could see several policemen gathered on the other side. Klodi grabbed Dad's arm and we crouched down behind some bushes and waited for them to walk away. My pulse thundered in my ears. What would they do if they caught us?

After several minutes, Klodi signaled us to follow him. When we reached the fence, I stared in disbelief. It must have been more than twice his height. Was he expecting us to climb over it?

Klodi scanned the bottom of the fence slowly with his flashlight and stopped where a small opening had been cut out. Thank God.

"Go through the hole," Klodi said. "Be careful. The wire is sharp around the edges."

Lowering my head, I slipped through and entered the parking area. Dad was right behind me.

Klodi pointed to the large red truck off to the right. "Go there."

He followed us but then stopped midway and watched for any signs of the police. We sped up and made it to the truck next to the one he had opened for us. Just as we were about to take the final couple of steps, I saw two figures coming our way with flashlights.

"Dad, the police!" I whispered.

Nodding, he pulled me down, and we crawled under the truck. The gravel and rough pavement tore into my hands and arms. We had lost Klodi.

The policemen stopped right next to us, their feet so close I could have touched them. One of them kicked an empty Coke can, and the other one kicked it back, starting a friendly soccer game I would have normally enjoyed watching. But not that night. Closing my eyes, I prayed that the can didn't roll under the truck, prompting them to search for it.

My neck hurt and I was cold, but I didn't dare make a sound. One mistake would send us to prison. They probably wouldn't lock up a child for long, but what about Dad? Would they hurt him? What if they took him away from us? And what would they do to Mom?

If I'd had a magic wand, I would have waved it over that entire nightmare and fled back to Albania as fast as I could. But I kept that to myself. I couldn't let Dad see my fears. I needed to keep his spirits up.

More footsteps. Another man. This one had red Adidas trainers—just like the ones I always dreamed of having. He didn't talk to anyone. He got into the truck and slammed the door. A few seconds later came a chortling, whirring, humming sound.

"What's that noise?" I whispered.

"He turned on the engine!"

A shiver ran down my spine. We were going to die under that truck! What could we do? If I screamed, the driver would stop the engine, but we would get caught. Who cared anymore? At least Dad and I would be safe.

I was about to scream when Dad grabbed my hand, slid out from under the truck, and pulled me hard. My knee scraped against a stone, and I felt a sharp pain. It was probably bleeding. I gasped for air.

"Shhh!" Dad placed his finger over his lips. "We can make it," he whispered. "Hide behind these tires. They can't see us here."

The two policemen spoke loudly to the driver, and the man turned off the engine and climbed out of the truck. They talked among themselves, and soon their voices grew fainter, as if they were walking away.

I concentrated harder, trying to understand what was going on. I couldn't hear them any longer. They must have left the parking area.

Dad peered out from behind the tires and nodded. "They're gone."

Klodi must have been hiding too because he suddenly reappeared. "You okay?" he whispered. "Come on, you need to get into the truck. The girl goes first."

Dad kissed my forehead. "Don't be afraid. I'll be right behind you."

While Dad directed the flashlight, Klodi lifted me up. "Place your feet on the edge and hold on to the bars," he said. "Climb up until you reach the top of the truck, and you'll see a small hole in the tarp. Put your head through it, and then shuffle along and allow your body to follow."

While Dad directed the flashlight, Klodi lifted me up. "Place your feet on the edge and hold on to the bars," he said. "Climb up until you reach the top of the truck, and you'll see a small hole we made in the tarp. Put your head through it, and then shuffle along and allow your body to follow."

Numb with terror, I followed Klodi's instructions, holding on to the bars and stepping carefully. If I hadn't been so scared, I would have thought it was a clever game. Someone was already inside—a young man named Aldi. He took hold of my head and shoulders, and I slipped in through the opening, just like a fish. Dad came through next, followed by two more people. It must have been hard for the adults to slip in. They were way too big to be fish.

Dad and I were very hungry but we couldn't eat. "The truck is full of cans of dog food," Aldi said. "I can tell you that for a fact because I tried to eat one." We made fun of him and started to laugh quietly, but I shuddered inwardly. I hadn't forgotten where I was.

Through the opening, Klodi said, "I'm going to close the truck. No more people. Gimi, you'll be leaving with one daughter. Your wife and other daughter will get into a different truck."

Dad's face turned dark with rage. "Absolutely not!" he hissed at Klodi. "If they don't get inside this truck, my daughter and I will leave."

Klodi sneered at him. "Better think twice about that, mister."

For sure, I wished we had never passed over the Italian borders.

That green-eyed officer. How I'd pleaded with him and prayed, never letting go of the Mother Mary figurine. But maybe it was nothing more than a figurine. Maybe Mother Mary didn't exist. Where was she? We needed her help. On top of everything going wrong, we couldn't possibly leave without Mom and Gita.

"There's nothing to think about," Dad said through clenched teeth. "You need to get my wife and other daughter. NOW."

"Okay, okay." Klodi sighed, holding up his hands and signaling to Dad to back off. "I'll get them."

He left and everyone fell silent. I counted my breaths—in and out, in and out. How many more breaths before Mom and Gita appeared?

What if the Albanians in charge took my mom and sister? What if they did something bad to them? Why were we separated in the first place? Did they have malicious plans for us? Who were those people? What made us trust them? What if this journey was all a lie? I would never forgive myself for leaving them behind.

For close to an hour, I tortured myself, counting eight hundred breaths of despair. And then Gita's head poked through the hole at the top of the truck. She was pulled through without making a sound. Mom slipped in after her. They were finally here.

"I love you both," I whispered countless times.

The French police had left the immediate area, so Klodi helped more people board the truck, bringing the total to thirteen. Next to us sat three young women with heavy makeup and revealing clothes. A young man in his early twenties was accompanying them. Mom and Dad looked at them and frowned.

From the guy's vague conversations with the women, we learned that his name was Niku and he was from Southern Albania. He had been in England before but had returned to Albania to bring the three women with him. From what I understood, he was setting up to be their pimp, to make money by selling them for prostitution.

"That's it," Niku whispered. "We can't let Klodi bring any more people. The risk of being caught is getting too high."

"Wait, wait! Eliza and me too." Hiesor called out as he popped his head into the truck.

"Shut your beak, you idiot!" Niku rasped. "The police are going to hear you, and they'll discover everyone else."

"I'm very sorry," Hiesor said. "Please, please, take us too."

"Quickly, we don't have time."

Hiesor shuffled into the truck and then stretched his arms to take the baby from Klodi, who had carried him up to the opening.

"No baby," Niku said, pushing Hiesor. "No way. We can't risk it. If the baby cries, the police will discover all of us."

Who put him in charge? Why wasn't Klodi saying anything?

"I promise he won't cry," Hiesor said. "Please, man, please."

"Okay, but if you get in, you'll have to leave the baby up to me. I'll make sure he doesn't cry. Otherwise, you can get out of the truck."

Hiesor nodded, and Niku backed down. Baby Eugen made it safely inside, and Eliza appeared after him.

"Now, give the baby this sleeping pill," Niku said to Eliza, a white tablet in his hand.

"What? I can't give that to my son," she said, her voice full of alarm. "He's only three months old. I don't even know what it is."

"Sorry," Niku said. "It's either the pill or the baby goes."

What did he mean by "the baby goes"?

Eliza glanced around at the rest of us, her eyes pleading for help. Dad whispered, "You don't have to give it to him."

Niku glared at him. "Shut the hell up! You don't know anything about this."

After a long, tense silence, Eliza's head and shoulders dropped in defeat, and she took the tablet. "I'll give him half."

I braced myself for Niku's reaction, but he didn't say a word.

Hiesor put his arm around his wife. "The baby will be all right."

Eliza broke the tablet in two and crushed one of the halves. Cradling Eugen in her arms, she licked her finger, dabbed it in the powder, and placed it in his mouth. And then she breastfed him. Tears running down her face, she did this again and again until the powder was gone.

It was close to two in the morning. More than an hour had passed since we'd gotten into the truck. By now, Klodi had probably finished helping the rest of the people leaving that night.

Packed in tightly, all sixteen of us sat still and quiet, staring at one another in the faint light seeping through the edges of the tarp. Baby Eugen was fast asleep.

Footsteps approached. Someone opened and closed the front door of the truck. The driver. He turned on the engine and the truck moved forward. After a few seconds, it slowed down and stopped.

Niku placed his finger over his lips, warning everyone to be quiet and not to lean on the tarp. I strained my ears to understand what was going on. More footsteps outside, followed by voices. Men, most likely police officers, were talking to the driver. They stood right next to the tarp—it was the only thing separating us.

One of the officers struck the tarp several times to see if anyone was inside. So that was why Niku warned us not to lean against it.

Then came the jangling of keys. Someone inserted a key into the truck's cargo lock and turned it. Just when I thought we had gotten away. This couldn't be happening. The police couldn't find us now! I shook from the cold, even though sweat was trickling down my forehead. I tried to swallow, but my mouth was too dry.

No one moved. I held on tightly to the Virgin Mary figurine. It would take only two seconds for them to catch all of us. Someone yelled from a distance. And more jangling. The police officer suddenly pulled the key out of the cargo lock and yelled back. It must have been important.

Inside the truck, a young man who understood French whispered in Albanian, "They have an urgent problem and need help."

Was that the truth? Was it something important or did more money change hands?

A few minutes later, the truck moved again. We looked at each other, counting the seconds. As the truck finally rolled onto the ferry, Dad gave a thumbs-up, an infectious smile spreading across his face.

Gita and I bit our hands so no one could hear our whispered scream, "Yes!"

We were off to England—this time for real.

PART TWO

England

CHAPTER 17

Refugees

Deti

July 31, 1999

I heard whispering and opened my eyes. To my right, Hiesor was studying a map of Kosovo and pronouncing the names of some streets. Next to me were shredded pieces of our Albanian passports. I lifted my head and saw Dad lost in thought.

"You didn't hide them well," I murmured to him.

It must have been close to six in the morning. A thick, foul smell filled the cramped truck. Throughout the night, many of the people urinated in the corner. The floor was wet. That, combined with sweaty, nervous body odor, made it hard not to gag.

I couldn't wait to breathe some fresh air.

Niku let us know that the truck had arrived in England, at the port of Folkestone. Everyone was focused. I got the feeling that the adults had been awake for a while or maybe they hadn't slept at all. In soft whispers, they reminded one another to tell the British authorities they were from Kosovo, as Klodi had advised, because Kosovars had a better chance of getting papers.

Outside, men's voices, gruff and coarse sounding. I was almost glad I couldn't understand what they were saying. But soon they were arguing, so something was wrong. I reached for Gita's hand and wove my fingers through hers. She squeezed my hand in return.

Now, footsteps and stomping, growing louder, more stomping, all clustered together. How many men were out there?

Inside the truck, all eyes were on Niku, who cut a flap-like opening in the side of the truck so when no police or immigration officers were nearby, we could climb out and run for it. After we escaped from the port officers, the plan was to take a train to London, a two-hour journey.

Niku hid his jackknife beneath one of the food cans and rubbed his hands together. All we could do now was wait. Carefully he pushed aside the flaps just enough to keep watch without being noticed.

Finally he turned away from his peephole and gave us a nod. "Now!" he whispered hoarsely, beckoning with his arm. "Go! And never speak English—otherwise they'll send you back home."

Niku was the first one to leave, followed by five guys scampering after him. We waited, Gita and I holding on to each other, right in front of Mom and Dad.

It was my turn. I let go of Gita's hand and pushed through the opening. But as soon as I landed on the pavement, the police swarmed the area, blowing their whistles and shouting. Everyone ran in all directions, screaming, pushing against each other, pushing against the chain enclosure.

A wave of panic rushed through me. Over my shoulder, I saw Mom, Gita, and Dad still in the truck. They hadn't even made it out. More and more police arrived, like they were falling out of the sky, and they ran after every person who tried to escape.

What should we do? What would happen to us? Gita, Mom, and Dad crawled out of the truck and joined me.

"This way, this way!" a policeman barked, a heavyset brute with a thick neck and shaved head.

No one moved. As Niku had instructed, I pretended I didn't understand what he was saying.

"Did you hear me?" the policeman snarled, this time louder. "This way, this way!"

Still no one moved. Gita and I were in this "no speak English" charade together. The policeman kept repeating the same words— how dumb could he be?

Behind us, Mom and Dad stood like statues, terrified.

"Fine, stay here." Mr. Brute shrugged. "What do you want to eat?" His eyes swept over us.

"I don't know," I said without thinking. Gita kicked my foot.

How could I have fallen for his trap?

"Aha! So you do speak English, don't you?" he glared at me.

"Numbers only," Gita said, and started counting loudly. "One, two, three, four, five . . ." She just saved me.

Mr. Brute grabbed his phone and was dialing when the chief policeman appeared. "Is the interpreter coming?"

"I'm calling her right now," Mr. Brute said. After exchanging a few words with the interpreter, he handed me the phone. "Talk to her."

The woman said a quick hello and then asked, "Where are you from?"

My knees felt weak. I wasn't ready for this. Why did I have to be the one to speak to her? So many grown-up Albanians were there, including my parents standing behind me. Why couldn't the police ask them?

I had no choice but to play along. I had to lie. There was no room for mistakes.

"Kosovo," I said, following Klodi's advice.

"Which part?"

I swallowed, gulped, swallowed again. I'd heard Mom and Dad talking about this possible question once or twice, but I hadn't paid any attention. And now I didn't have an answer. I couldn't cheat and ask Mom and Dad either. The policeman would doubt us even more. But no way was I going to surrender. I needed to buy some time and think carefully.

"I'm sorry, I didn't hear you." Did she notice the quiver in my voice? "Could you please repeat what you said?"

The interpreter spoke loudly and clearly. "Which part of Kosovo do you come from?"

Ah, yes, I remembered! "Prishtina."

Without acknowledging my response, the interpreter moved on

to the next question mechanically, totally indifferent to what we were all going through. "What do you want to eat?"

"Anything. I don't care." I emphasized each word with the Kosovo accent I had never practiced before, but it worked better than I could have imagined. I was beginning to be a real Kosovo girl.

It's funny how life catches you unexpectedly, how when you get stuck, when the bar is raised in front of you, and you have to jump really high—really high!—to get over it. Yes, that is the real test of life, the test that separates winners from losers, the strong from the weak. I was jumping high, I was strong, and for the moment, I was winning.

The conversation lasted no more than five minutes. I managed to stay in the game with no falls, no off sides, no penalties.

Mr. Brute took the phone from me and pointed. "Inside," he said.

Reluctantly, Mom, Dad, Gita, and I followed the rest of the group into a prison-like building, where a policeman led us to a small room. As soon as we entered, everyone crowded around me. I was now a celebrity because I had spoken to the interpreter. Did I have any news? What did the policemen say? What did the interpreter ask?

A tall man with a large belly wagged his finger at me. "You better tell us."

I winced at his fierce tone. "Nothing... nothing important, except that the interpreter wanted to know where I came from."

"That's extremely important. What did you say?"

"Kosovo."

"Good girl," the man said.

The rest of the group nodded in approval. Gita and my parents moved into the corner, apart from everyone else. I started to join them, but another man grabbed my arm.

"Did they ask you anything else?" he asked.

"What I wanted to eat."

"All right. That's not important."

This time I managed to break away from them and go over to my family. Dad was stomping his feet. That meant he was nervous.

He wasn't the only one.

Several of the people started pacing from one end of the small room to the other. Some closed their eyes as if trying to escape, while others stared dully as if they had already given up.

The minutes ticked by. Each one felt like an hour.

The door opened and a short policewoman entered the room. "Hiesor and Eliza, would you please follow us?" She gestured to make them understand.

Gita turned to Dad. "What's going to happen now?"

Before he could answer, another policewoman opened the door. "Mr. Zalli and family, please follow me."

We shuffled behind her down a narrow hall to another cell. She pulled out a set of keys from her pocket, opened the heavy door, and waved us through. After saying something in English, she closed the door and left.

"What did she say?" Mom asked. She and Dad both looked worried.

I shook my head. I didn't understand a word and neither did Gita. It was the strangest English I'd ever heard.

So there we sat on the cold, bare floor of the tiny cell. And sat and sat. And yet . . . we were still in England, still holding on. My head was pounding. I closed my eyes and leaned back against the wall just as the door opened and a third policewoman entered, this time with a tray holding four white plastic bowls. "Something for you to eat," she said.

Curious, I uncovered my bowl. Rice with vegetables—the first time I'd seen rice cooked that way. I poked my fork into it and place a morsel on my tongue. It was odd but not bad.

"You should finish all of it," Mom said.

I sighed and placed another forkful in my mouth, forcing myself to eat. I had no appetite. Gita finished hers quietly. Mom and Dad didn't touch theirs.

⤝◈⤞

Worn out, we all dozed off and on. Hours later, we heard footsteps approaching. One of the large policemen we saw earlier opened the door. His huge shadow covered most of the opposite wall. "Mr. Zalli, come with me. You too, Mrs. Zalli. Don't worry, girls, they will be back shortly." Since he didn't know we spoke English, he gestured with his hands, trying to reassure us.

Mom and Dad gave us a quick smile, not at all comforting because we knew how worried they were. Their footsteps echoed in the hall, growing fainter until we could no longer hear them.

"Please, God, help us," I said. "Make everything go all right."

We waited and waited, each of us taking turns walking around the small room.

"They must be asking Mom and Dad a lot of questions," I said, sitting back down next to Gita. "Do you think they're going to be okay?" My voice broke as I struggled to hold back the tears.

"Don't be silly. They're just fine." Gita gently rubbed my arm. I laid my head on her knees and she put her arm around me.

An hour later, footsteps again. The same policeman ushered Dad inside and left without saying anything. Dad shuffled in, exhausted. His unshaven face made him look older and his eyes were red. Had he been crying? He slid down to the floor and slumped forward.

"What happened?" Gita asked softly.

Whatever Dad had to tell us couldn't be good. Instead of answering Gita's question, he asked, "Has Mom not been back yet?"

"No. Wasn't she with you? Do you know where she is?"

"They must still be interrogating her."

"What did they ask you?"

"Where I was from."

"And you told them that we come from Prishtina?"

"Well, I tried." Dad swiped the back of his hand over his eyes. "But it wasn't easy, considering that they hired an interpreter—a guy named Dardan—who happened to be from Prishtina. He was a nasty surprise. It didn't take him long to figure out we weren't from Kosovo."

"But he—"

The arrival of a policewoman with Mom interrupted my question. The woman let go of Mom's arm as she opened the door and then immediately closed it behind her.

Mom looked as terrible as Dad. "Gimi, they spotted the truth. They realized I wasn't from Kosovo. They told me to admit that I had lied. And I did."

"Don't worry, honey, they caught me too." Dad sighed. "It was all Dardan's bloody fault."

"You mean the interpreter?"

"Sure. He wanted to know exactly where we lived in Prishtina. The names of any shops, streets, schools. I knew nothing." He dropped his head in his hands. "What's done is done. What will be will be. We tried our best."

He grew silent, and we huddled together, fearing the worst. When the policewoman returned, she said, "Zalli family, please follow me. This is the last time." That must mean they were sending us back to Albania. I was too worn out to care.

But she led us to yet another room, where a middle-aged blond woman sat at a table, welcoming us with a warm smile. Surely, she wasn't about to give us bad news.

"This is where I was," Dad whispered.

Leaning on the same table was a man with Mediterranean-Albanian features. "Come inside," he said in Kosovo Albanian. "Make yourselves comfortable." He had to be Dardan, the interpreter. He nodded toward the woman as if he were giving her permission to continue.

"Hello, girls, how are—" She stopped and looked at us, her eyes wide. "Oh, my gosh. Am I seeing double? Are you really twins?"

We giggled, understanding everything she said, but we weren't sure whether we still needed to pretend we couldn't speak English.

"Are you two twins?" Dardan asked in Albanian.

"Yes, they are," Dad said. "And they speak English."

Dardan translated for the woman. "Oh, I see," she said. "That's great to be able to speak at this early age." She nodded in approval. "So you must be identical twins?"

"Yes," we both answered.

"I really can't tell you two apart. What's the difference?"

"There is no difference in identical twins," I said.

"I already see a difference. You must be the loud one."

I smiled. "I was talking about the physical difference, ma'am."

"I'm sure I can come up with something, but you have to give me a bit of time." She had lost interest in the business at hand and was now in the world of twin sisters.

Dardan looked annoyed as he watched the three of us conversing amiably. That gave Gita and me much pleasure, especially after everything we had gone through. Standing tall and straight, we waited for the woman to identify us. Mom and Dad had already told her our names.

After a few minutes, she broke the silence. "Oh, I give up. What's the difference? Please tell me." She laughed.

"I have a mole on my right cheek," I said.

"Let me see." She stood and leaned forward. "Ah, so there is a physical difference. Why didn't you tell me?"

"Well, you know, I like to test people."

"That's very cheeky!" The woman smiled. "Are you Argita or Detina? And I guess you must be the older one too."

"Wrong guess. I'm Detina, the younger one. But that doesn't mean I'm not the bossy one."

The woman laughed. "So how much younger than your twin are you?"

"At least five minutes."

"Is that true?" She turned to Gita, as if she didn't trust me.

"Well, not really. I'm only three minutes older, but Deti makes me out to be much older than I actually am, since she really wants to be the baby of the family. But she isn't really. I mean, we're twins. We're the same."

The woman laughed again, clicking her tongue against her teeth. At least for a moment we were able to relieve some of the pressure. "Oh, girls, you made my day!"

She looked down at some papers in front of her and asked for the correct spelling of our names and our dates of birth. On July 31, 1999, at midnight, we stopped lying. We were thirteen years old. We were ourselves again.

The woman jotted down her final notes while Mom pressed her fingers onto an ink pad and then rolled them on a piece of paper, leaving a clean impression. Dardan explained that the police were taking her fingerprints. As soon as Mom finished, Gita and I did the same thing.

"Okay then, we're done." The woman handed a green piece of paper to Dad. At the top was printed "IND," and our names and dates of birth were written underneath. She told us that IND—the Immigration Nationality Directorate—was part of the Home Office, a department of the United Kingdom government.

Gita and I studied the paper. On the top right-hand side was written "Gran Canaria, Marine Parade 4 to 7, Folkestone CT20 1PX," the name and address of the hotel where we were supposed to stay. And at the bottom was the address of Social Services, where we needed to go every Tuesday, the woman said. There was also an expiration date of August 31, 1999. What did that mean?

At least for now, we didn't have to worry about all the details. Dardan was translating everything to Dad, who nodded, indicating he understood.

My heart lifted for the first time in days. Exhausted, hungry, and filthy, we had officially arrived.

CHAPTER 18

Our New Family

Gita

August 1, 1999

When I woke up the next morning, I took in every detail of the small hotel room: the windows, curtains, chairs, bunk beds, night table. Yes, it looked real enough. Albania was somewhere in the corner of my mind, a distant geographical region on the map. The room was cold. I snuggled into the warm brown blanket of England and let the entire country embrace me. We were here at last. It felt so good, so right and safe.

Mom and Dad were already awake, talking in whispers to keep from waking us.

"Gimi, we should buy a phone card and call the family, especially my mom. I'm sure they must be worried. They haven't heard from us in days."

They saw that I was awake and greeted me with lovely smiles. Deti stirred and rolled over. "What time is it?" she asked sleepily.

I looked over at the clock, an ancient fixture hanging on the wall.

"It's almost eight-thirty," Mom said. Her tone was all business. "Hurry and wash up, both of you! Remember, last night you said the breakfast room closed at nine."

"Breakfast in the breakfast room." Deti enunciated each word slowly as she sat up and stretched, grinning over at me. She was probably thinking the same thing I was. When did we ever have breakfast served to us in Albania?

It didn't take long for us to get ready. Eagerly we followed Mom and Dad down the corridor to the main part of the hotel.

Dad pulled open the heavy brass handle on the breakfast room door and smiled as we swept past him into the room, Deti's eyes wide with amazement. I wished I'd had the camera right then. I would have given anything to capture her expression. There was so much to take in—neither of us knew where to look first. The soft crimson-colored carpet, artistically configured with tiny flowers, was very modern. In front of us, rows of tables were neatly set with sparkling silverware and starched white napkins. It was all so elegant, so . . . so English.

At 8:50, we were the only guests, but crumbs on the floor suggested other people had already had their breakfast. A hushed air of expectancy hovered over the room. We chose a corner table by the window that looked out onto the street—a British street!—and gingerly we sat down, careful not to disturb anything. I was afraid to upset even the smallest detail of the table setting. It was so perfect, so exquisite.

"So what do we do now, Dad?" Deti said.

It all seemed like a dream. There we were, the four of us, sitting in a posh restaurant, about to be served breakfast without paying for it, when less than twenty-four hours ago we were hiding inside a truck with nothing to eat. Our parents always said that no one gives you anything for free. What was the catch? What was really going on here?

"We'll wait until someone comes and takes our order." Dad smiled at her. He turned to me and tapped my hand reassuringly, but I knew that like me, he was experiencing the unreality of it all.

The white door separated the restaurant from the kitchen groaned as it was pushed open and a short olive-skinned woman with Mediterranean features came into the room. "Oh dear, oh, I'm so sorry. You wait long?" She bustled over to our table, glancing nervously at each of us, and then fixed her eyes on Dad.

"No, don't worry," I said.

"She is even apologizing to us," Deti said in Albanian to Mom.

The waitress swiveled around and briskly went back through the groaning white door. A few moments later, she reappeared with two small white plates of toast balanced on each of her palms and placed them on the table. "You full breakfast, yes?" she asked in broken English, pointing at Dad and then at Mom.

Mom and Dad turned frantically to us. "Girls, can you translate what she's saying?"

"She is asking what you want to eat," I said. "You need to say yes."

"Yes, yes!" Mom smiled at the woman.

The woman smiled in return. "Two breakfasts and two cornflakes." Again she disappeared.

I shook my head, confused. "But she never asked Deti or me what we wanted to eat. What are cornflakes?"

"They must be some kind of chocolate," Deti said.

I clapped my hands. "Chocolate!"

"At least someone came to take our order." A satisfied Deti pushed back her chair, went over to Dad, and planted a kiss on his forehead.

Just as I was wondering what our next surprise would be, the breakfast room door handle jiggled. I glanced toward the entrance, pretending to be indifferent, but I'm more than a little curious to learn who else was staying there. When the door opened, a little girl probably no older than four, with curly blond hair and a Disney Cinderella dress, barreled into the restaurant. Following her was a well-built man in a tight-fitting T-shirt that showed off his perfect physique. Thick muscles bulged beneath his sleeves.

"Dad, Dad, I don't want to eat breakfast," the little girl said in Albanian. She laughed and toddled around the restaurant, waving her arms.

"Come here, Kristina," the man said, also in Albanian. "You'll fall and hurt yourself." He chased after her and scooped her up in his arms as if she were a tiny doll. "You and your sister are Dad's big pride." He sat at a table near ours.

Then came a young woman with long black hair carrying a girl who looked a couple of years younger than her sister. The little girl covered her face with her hands and peeked out at us through her fingers.

An Albanian family! In the midst of a strange and awkward English setting, we were blessed with the familiar.

Mom's eyes were shining. She smiled broadly and nudged Dad to go say hello.

Dad pushed back his chair and went over to them. "Hello, how are you?" he said in Albanian.

"Oh, hello!" The man stood and shook Dad's hand heartily. "We've been wanting to make some Albanian friends for months, but we haven't come across any. We are really glad to meet you." Both he and his wife nodded warmly.

Mom joined them and we followed.

"My wife, Dita, and our daughters, Gita and Deti," Dad said.

"So nice to meet all of you. I am Bani and this is my wife, Mira, and these are our daughters, Kristina and Pami. Your accent tells me you're from the south."

"That's correct. We come from Fier. You too, must be from the south—at least your accent is very southern."

"Yes, my friend, I am from Vlorë."

"So how long have you been living here?"

"It has been almost three months, hasn't it, Mira?"

"Well, to be precise, we came on the fourth of May," Mira said. "We live in room 122, on the third floor. We would love it if you could visit us." She smiled brightly at all four of us.

"We certainly will," Mom said. "It's good to know that we aren't the only Albanians in the hotel."

Strangers become crucial in moments when you're feeling alone, drowning in all the confusion and uncertainties of a foreign country. A kind word is worth a thousand gestures.

The groaning door let us know that the waitress was coming toward our table. The shabby cloth she held beneath the hot breakfast plates to protect her hands ruined the perfect image of her high-quality service.

"Breakfast ready," she called out in a high-pitched voice.

When everyone was seated again, the waitress placed Mom's and

Dad's breakfast plates in front of them, accompanied by a series of elaborate hand gestures in an attempt to make her English more understandable. "This for you, this for you."

"Camilla, get your two cornflakes out of the way, please!" a gruff male voice called from the kitchen.

Camilla rushed back to the kitchen and returned with a tray bearing two bowls and another rack of toast. "This for you, this for you." She placed each of the bowls in front of Deti and me.

"Thank you very much indeed," we both said to her back as she hurried away.

I stared down at the bowl of yellowish-orange bits. "Deti, dear, taste your chocolate."

Deti made a face at me. We dipped our spoons into the bits and tasted them. Whatever they were, we weren't convinced we wanted to eat them. But Camilla had given us no choice.

We gazed longingly at our parents' plates, each with a fried egg, two sausages, baked beans, bacon, fried bread, and hash brown potatoes. Without a word, Mom and Dad removed portions of their breakfast and placed them on the two toast plates.

Our first English breakfast.

The next morning, we were treated to another wonderful surprise when Hiesor, Eliza, and baby Eugen entered the breakfast room.

Mom and Eliza cried tears of joy and relief when they saw each other. Mom and Dad introduced Hiesor and Eliza to Bani and Mira while Deti and I took turns holding little Eugen.

This was our new family. Now that we knew there were other Albanians in the hotel, people in the same situation we could share our problems with, life seemed safer and more serene—at least for now.

CHAPTER 19

Believe and Hold On

Gita

August 9, 1999

As we entered the breakfast room, we spotted Hiesor and Eliza at the middle table, their heads bent low. Baby Eugen was fussing in Eliza's arms, but his parents were engrossed in a serious conversation and trying to ignore him.

"Something must be going on," Dad said. He went over to chat with them, hoping to bring some cheer. Mom, Deti, and I followed closely behind.

"How are you?" Dad asked with a big smile.

Hiesor turned away from his wife and looked at us. His young face was drawn, dark circles under his eyes.

Dad's smile faded. "What's wrong? What is it?"

Hiesor shook his head. "Bad news, I'm afraid." He picked up his IND from the table and handed it to Dad. "This is the problem."

"I don't understand."

"We met with Bani last night." Hiesor's voice trembled. "And by chance, we happened to see his IND . . ."

"And? Come on, man, don't keep me waiting."

"Bani's IND says he has the right to stay in England for two years. My IND is completely different. Look at it. Our permission to stay ends in three weeks."

"Is this what you're worried about?" Dad face relaxed. "We both have the same IND. I don't think that's what it means, but I can ask for you if you like. We're going to Social Services tomorrow. There's no point in panicking, Hiesor. This shouldn't be a big deal."

Hiesor slammed his fist on the table, his eyes filled with angry tears. He drew in a deep breath. "Yes, this is a very big deal. It's just the way we predicted it. We told them the truth, and they answered as we thought they would. They'll send us Albanians back to our country. We made a big mistake. We should have stayed with our story that we were from Kosovo. If we had done that, we'd be able to stay here."

Dad glanced over at Eliza and back at Hiesor. "Try to calm down, both of you. We're going to figure this out tomorrow."

"We can't wait that long. We're leaving for Ireland this afternoon. I threw all my money away trying to get to England, and I can't afford to go back to Albania. I'm broke. I won't be able to keep my family there."

Eliza chewed her nails, a tear trickling down her face. If the situation was that serious for Hiesor and Eliza, it was just as serious for us.

Hiesor reached into the pocket of his jeans and drew out a piece of paper. "Here's my number. Call me if you decide to join us."

Mom, Deti, and I leaned down to put our arms around Eliza. With difficulty she stood, handed the baby to Hiesor, and gratefully hugged us back.

I flashed back to Albania. Once more, the sirens, the crackling of the bullets filled my ears. Armed men tearing into our courtyard, the beach bus, our schools, our lives.

All of this seemed so beautiful, so peaceful. Was it just a mirage?

If Hiesor was right, where would we go? What would we do?

Mom's and Dad's eyes grew dark with worry. Even though we were still considered children, Deti and I were quickly becoming adults, expected now to help our parents understand and solve all our problems. Our journey to England had cost a huge amount of money. If we were already in debt, how on earth would we survive if British Immigration sent us back to Albania? Dad had lost his job. If we didn't return the loan within two years and start to replenish our savings that went toward our immigration fee, what would happen to us?

So many questions.

There was nothing more to say. Sometimes silence is the loudest scream of all. Quietly Eliza reached for the baby, taking him from Hiesor's arms as if he were the only possession she still had. Sensing his mother's despair, Eugen started to cry. The intensity of his wails marked the gravity of our conversation. With a quick kiss, we said good luck and goodbye.

Within seconds, they made their way out of the restaurant and disappeared into their own world, which, like ours, was now riddled with even more problems than before.

"Don't worry, girls," Dad said, speaking softly. "Nothing bad is going to happen. All of that is nothing but gossip. We're going to be fine, I promise. We have to hope that good things are coming our way."

His words sounded hollow. Wasn't there always some truth in gossip?

But as I thought about our situation, I realized we had two choices: spend a lot of time worrying and making ourselves feel worse than we already did or, like Dad, choose to be optimistic. He was right. Hope was all we had to cling to. Hope and faith—the two guiding forces that had brought us this far. We couldn't afford to lose either.

The next day, Deti and I went with Mom and Dad to Social Services and asked about the IND date. No one could help us there—we needed to contact the Home Office—but they did give us a small amount of money for food, clothing, and transportation. It broke our hearts, but we had to accept that we would never see our suitcases again. Klodi had no way of knowing where we were, even if he had told us the truth, which was doubtful. All we had were the clothes on our backs.

Before we left Albania, Dad had talked to someone with a contact in London. Luckily, I had memorized his phone number, and Dad called him. Happy to help, Ladi told Dad about his attorney, Ikie, who worked pro bono on Saturdays. Deti and I talked to him right away and scheduled an appointment for that weekend.

Using the money from Social Services, all four of us took the train to London and went directly to Ikie's office. He was the first Black person we had ever seen and the first Black person we had ever shaken hands with. Born in Africa, he had experience emigrating to England. We explained our situation, and he said he would do his best to get an extension before August 31 arrived.

A week later, still no word from Hiesor and Eliza. Did they make it to Ireland? Had they been sent back to Albania? No news from Ikie either. We waited, each day melting into the next.

Finally, a letter arrived one morning from the Home Office addressed to Dad. We all sat around the small table in our room while Deti translated it. Dad needed to go to Dover to have his fingerprints taken, the letter said. The Home Office had forgotten that detail. It all seemed rather routine, just an administrative slip-up—but was there something more to it?

Mom glanced nervously at Dad. "Maybe Hiesor was right. We should have gone to Ireland too." She ran her fingers distractedly through her hair. "What does it matter anymore? The handwriting is on the wall."

"Well, Dita, we don't know why they need the fingerprints," Dad said with his usual optimism.

"Gimi, can't you see? They're going to return you to Albania."

"We don't know that for sure, do we?"

"It's not hard to imagine, is it?"

Dad rose from his chair. "Girls, come with me. Let's go talk to Don Carlos. Surely, he knows more about this than we do."

Don Carlos was from Spain. A short, chubby man probably in his fifties, judging from his salt-and-pepper hair, although his round face made him look younger. During the past two weeks we had been residing at the Gran Canaria Hotel, he had been kind to us, eagerly helping the refugees Social Services paid him to accommodate at his hotel. It was in his best interest to be friendly to his guests so they would take care of their rooms.

In the mornings Don Carlos usually worked at the front desk. When we approached him, he was hanging up the phone. "So, Mr. Zalli, how can I help you?" He nodded and smiled.

"You know what to say, don't you?" Dad asked me in Albanian. This time it was my turn to translate and Deti's job to make sure I was correct.

"Yes, Dad."

Deti and I often talked to Don Carlos in Italian or English. And sometimes our conversation was a mixture of the two: English-Italian.

"Don Carlos, would you please look at this letter? We think it's bad news. That they're going to return my dad to Albania."

He skimmed it. "Oh, no, there's nothing going on, girls." He smiled reassuringly at Dad. "Don't worry, Mr. Zalli. It is not what you think. They just forgot to take your fingerprints. They are definitely not going to return you to Albania."

Don Carlos turned to me. "This is a simple procedure they do with everyone. Trust me, you are going to be fine, and—"

"Are you sure?" Deti interrupted.

"I'm positive. You don't have to worry. You will be fine."

Greatly relieved, Dad shook Don Carlos's hand. When we returned to our room, Mom was already at the door when we opened it. "So, Gimi, what did he say?" She searched his face anxiously.

"Good news. I have to go to Dover tomorrow morning with one of the girls, and they'll take my fingerprints. They do it with everyone who comes into this country. They did it with you, remember? And now it's my turn."

Dad smiled and kissed my head, as if rewarding me for doing such a good job as interpreter. Don Carlos had lifted his spirits.

The next morning came too soon. I snuggled under the blanket and partially opened my eyes. Dad and Deti were already gone. I hadn't heard them leave. I must have fallen into a deep sleep.

"Wake up, honey." Mom emerged from the bathroom where she

was washing clothes. The wet laundry dripped onto the floor. She hung each item on a small plastic hanger and then came over to cuddle me with the sweetest words only moms know.

"It's almost nine o'clock, sleepyhead. If we want to have some breakfast, we have to go downstairs now. Quickly, go to the bathroom, brush your teeth, and let's get going."

I let out a groan. It was hard to resist the magical feeling of staying warm in bed. It was chilly. Even so, I followed Mom's instructions and we were off to have some breakfast.

Afterward, we locked ourselves inside the hotel room and talked about Albania, about Grandma and Grandpa, uncles, aunties, cousins, friends, and all the beautiful times we'd had back home. Now it seemed as though we never really appreciated the beauty of those days until we arrived in England.

The time flew by, and when we both looked at the clock, it was three o'clock. We had talked away the morning and most of the afternoon. Dad and Deti should be returning any moment. Why were they late? After all, they were only going to Dover, which, according to Don Carlos, was less than an hour away from Folkestone. They left at seven. That was eight hours ago.

Another hour passed. Something must be wrong. Mom's deep sigh reflected her own fears. "Mom, it's nearly four o'clock. Why aren't they back yet?"

"Well, it could be for several reasons," she said, sounding like she was talking more to herself than to me. "Maybe the appointment time was changed . . . maybe they needed an interpreter . . . maybe they—"

"Are you telling me you're not worried?" I interrupted her, a quiver in my voice.

"Well, let's give them another ten minutes, shall we?"

More waiting. That's all we seemed to do in England. I imagined hearing the door handle click. In my mind's eye, I saw the quick, sudden movement of the door opening—and there they were, casting away all my fears.

A quick phone call would have been so good, just to let us know they were safe. What could have happened? Had they been sent back to Albania? Or something a lot worse?

"C'mon, Mom, let's go see Don Carlos."

At once, she got up and grabbed my arm. Her patience had run out too.

Don Carlos stood at the reception desk, jotting down notes in his big blue book. He looked tired, his eyes red beneath his glasses. He had probably been working for several hours. As soon as he saw our faces, he knew something was wrong.

"Are you okay, Mrs. Zalli? What about you, Gita? But of course you are not," he added hastily. "Please tell me what is wrong."

Don Carlos removed his glasses and placed them on the desk as if to separate himself from his work so he could give us his full attention.

"Go on, Gita, explain the situation to him." Mom rubbed my shoulders, encouraging me.

"Don Carlos, do you remember when we showed you that letter from Dover saying that my dad had to go to the Home Office because they had to take his fingerprints?" My voice was so weak and thin with anxiety Don Carlos was having trouble understanding me.

He frowned for a moment, then finally waved his hand, his eyes clearing. "Ah, yes, and what is the problem with this, dear?"

"The problem is that my dad and Deti left at seven this morning and they're not back yet. Who knows what could have happened to them?" I studied his face, looking for some kind of reassurance that nothing was wrong after all. As if Don Carlos would know that everything was all right when he didn't have any more information about Dad and Deti than we did.

I fought back the tears, no longer caring about being sent back to Albania. All I cared about were Dad and Deti and the four of us being together. Mrs. England had already shown us how tough she was, and I wouldn't let her destroy my whole life.

Don Carlos came closer and touched my hand. "Nothing has

happened, believe me. They are fine and they should be back soon. Come on, let's get into my car and I will drive around to see whether they're nearby."

How kind of him. Gratefully I nodded. Mom clutched my hand and held on to it tightly as we followed Don Carlos to his car.

As he drove through the streets, the two of us anxiously gazed out the windows looking for a medium-height man and teenage girl with dark hair. No trace of them anywhere.

"What if some stranger killed them?" Mom, who an hour ago seemed so strong, started to weep. "Why the hell did I come here? Deti, where are you? What has happened to you? Why are you not coming home?"

My insides started shaking. I hated it when Mom did this. "Stop it, will you?" I raised my voice. "Why do you make things worse? I will never forgive you if your awful words bring bad luck."

Oh how I wished Mom were wrong. She must be mistaken, she must be. They were fine, but what if . . .

Mom leaned back in the seat and fell silent, holding her head in her hands.

"I will just pull up here." Don Carlos stopped in front of a large gray building. His face was somber. Even though we were speaking Albanian, he didn't have to understand us to know how terrified we were, and now he was on edge too. "Ladies, come with me. We will ask about this at the police station."

I stared at the building as Don Carlos opened the back door and we climbed out. Did this mean that Mom might be right after all? Did Don Carlos now think the situation was critical, that something bad had happened to Dad and Deti after all? Would it be only Mom and me here in England? Was that it? How would we live? Who was doing this to us?

Even though it was past five o'clock, two police officers were behind the desk. A young overweight man with glasses recorded our story in a notebook. An older police woman, maybe in her fifties, smiled at us as Don Carlos helped us answer their questions.

I told the officers about Dad's appointment and when he and Deti left. And I described them both, including as many details as possible.

"We haven't come across any accidents or missing cases over the last twelve hours," the police officer said, looking up from his notebook. "If they don't appear by tomorrow morning, come back again."

Tomorrow morning? How could we wait that long?

Don Carlos walked around the town with us, past the city hall and many shops, and through the parks. We asked passersby, merchants, even little children if they had seen a middle-aged man and thirteen-year-old girl.

The answers were the same: "Sorry, we can't help you."

Don Carlos stopped walking and turned to us. "Do not worry, ladies. I am sure they are okay and they will be back soon. Let's go back to the hotel and wait for them to show up. At this point, it is the only thing left to do."

In the back seat of the car, tightly holding my hands, Mom leaned forward to kiss my head. "Be strong," she said.

Her words infuriated me. Of the two of us, who had fallen apart, sobbing hysterically and carrying on? "You're telling me to be strong?" I shouted at her. "What about you? I promise you, nothing has happened to them. They're fine." I couldn't stand it when Mom went over the edge. We couldn't drag each other down like that.

On the way back to the hotel, neither of us spoke. Don Carlos parked the car and turned off the engine. Wordlessly we got out, waiting for him to lock the doors.

Suddenly he let out a loud laugh. What was wrong with him? Why was he laughing? I glared at him, angry and disappointed. This was surely not a time to laugh.

Don Carlos pointed at the front door of the hotel. "Isn't that your dad?"

My heart beat faster. It was Dad and Deti!

"Dad!" I called out and raced toward him, jumping into his arms and hugging him tightly. He was back again. It was so good feeling him close to me. The tears ran freely down my face and I didn't care.

Mom squeezed Deti's arm. "I thought something bad had happened to you, and I would have never forgiven myself for that."

Dad seemed to be totally oblivious to all the drama.

"Dad, where have you been?" I asked. "We've been looking for you all over town."

"Yes, yes, I am so sorry, baby, but we didn't have a choice. Let's go upstairs and talk about it." He reached out to Mom. "Are you all right, Dita?"

Mom still hadn't said a word to him. Her eyes shot darts at him. "How can you ask me that?" she snapped. "Do you have any idea what we have been through during the last hours? Why the hell didn't you call us?"

"Well, because we don't have a phone, do we?"

"That's true, we don't, but the hotel does. Couldn't you have taken the number and left a message with Don Carlos?'

Dad put his arms around her, hugging her tightly. Mom stifled a sob and struggled for self-control as she clung to him. Deti and I hugged both of them from behind.

Mom's anger vanished and so did mine. It didn't matter why they were late. What was important was that we were all together again and hugging each other.

Mom pulled away and let out a long sigh. "Okay, you two, tell us what happened."

Dad and Deti had a story all right. Someone had told them that Dover was about thirty minutes away, so they walked to save the bus fare. With so little money, even the smallest amount we could save was a big help. Dad said that since they didn't know where the Home Office was located, they ended up along the narrow shoulder of the busy motorway as the cars sped past them. It was a long and dusty walk—they even saw snakes coming out of the bushes. They were terrified.

Five hours later—five hours it took them!—they reached the Home Office in Dover.

CHAPTER 20

A Dream Come True

Deti

October 5, 1999

Gita and I called Ikie every morning, probably driving him crazy, though he always sounded kind and patient. When the end of August came and went and we still hadn't received any news from the Home Office, it was impossible to think we would be able to stay in England.

Would they grab us off the street while we were walking? Every time we left the hotel, I glanced over my shoulder, thinking today would be the day we were deported.

Then in late September, Ikie had good news. The Home Office extended our IND, expiring now at the end of January. This took the edge off our worry, but it was hard not to think about the clock ticking.

During our first two months in England, we were introduced to both the sweet and sour sides of our new world. All the Albanians staying in the hotel were now gone. A week after Hiesor left, Bani and his family went to visit their friends in London. We missed them.

Maybe this was because Gita and I didn't have any friends other than Mom and Dad. We went out with them almost every day, and when no one was around, we picked blackberries from the bushes at the corner of Marina Parade Street. Mom bought a mini electric cooker for the hotel room, and she made delicious blackberry jam— no need to buy it at the store.

I liked going food shopping with Mom and Dad. We picked up cheese, butter, baked beans, and bread—just the basics and always economy food. Gita and I never asked for chocolates or croissants or any other treats, but Dad sometimes bought Cokes for us. He said they weren't expensive, so Gita and I didn't have to count how many times each of us took a sip.

During one of our trips to get groceries, we discovered a laundromat close to the hotel. We started going there once a week, and Mom did hand washing in our room on the other days because we didn't have a lot of clothes.

On Sundays, we walked to a farmers market about five minutes from the hotel. Everything was cheap and got even cheaper at four o'clock just before they started packing up. Dad said they had to get rid of the produce, so they slashed their prices. We bought a big box of bananas for one pound, cheaper than in Albania. Every time Uncle Kutbi bought me a banana, I kept it like a treasure. Now, I could eat as many as I wanted.

Back at our hotel, we had a magical view from our window: the massive Rotunda Amusement Park. So many amazing rides. It gave me such joy to watch all the kids having fun, especially on Saturdays and Sundays when it got extra busy. Maybe we would all go there one day too.

Apart from running errands with Mom and Dad, Gita and I spent most of our time inside the hotel room. We played, we fought, we kissed and made up, and we got bored too—especially when we went to the Social Services office to translate for our parents and other refugees. People had so many problems and we had to listen carefully so we could translate fairly. It gave me a headache, these grown-up responsibilities.

Gita and I took turns on who would translate on which day. Sometimes I made her believe it was her turn even if it wasn't. She was more patient than I was.

How I wished I could improve my English. September had already passed, and I missed school. Learning had always been a passion for

Gita and me, even when we were young, just like it was for Mom and Dad. We couldn't wait to go to an English school.

Gita

October 18, 1999

A few days ago, Don Carlos stopped by with the best news. He'd called all the secondary schools in Folkestone, and the Channel School had room for us—provided we passed the English language test.

Now Deti and I were sitting in the back seat of Don Carlos's car, Dad in the passenger seat, on our way to the school to take the test. We would see an English school for the first time. My stomach fluttered with nerves and excitement. We had no idea what to expect. Would the school be like I dreamed it would be? Would the test be difficult? Would we pass? Would they register us?

When we pulled into the parking lot, I got a good view of the school. It was huge. The campus actually consisted of several buildings, unlike the single buildings in Albania. The only word I could think of to describe it was "posh," one of the new English words I had learned. As we walked toward the entrance, I counted four large green fields where students practiced sports.

"Gita, everyone is wearing a uniform!" Deti grabbed my arm, her eyes wide.

She was right. Black shoes, gray trousers, a white shirt, a tie, and a reddish-brown top with the school's name on it. Next to us were two tall girls, standing straight and proper. They even wore makeup. Although we were careful not to look directly at them, we couldn't help stealing sideways glances.

Opposite the main entrance was a large dining area. I pictured students eating different kinds of meals, anything they wanted—even dessert. The hallway was clean and the classrooms spacious. Peeking through the small windows, we saw plenty of desks and chairs—we always seemed to be short of both in Albania—and two large whiteboards at the front of every classroom.

"Come on, girls," Don Carlos called out from the end of the hall-way, where he waited with Dad. "It's past nine o'clock. The test is about to start. We should not be late!"

We hurried along, scarcely able to stop looking around us. Com-pared to Hekuran Maneku School in Patos, where we had studied for the past seven years, the Channel School was a palace. No broken bricks, broken walls, broken chairs. And we wouldn't get slivers in our hands from touching rough, unpainted classroom doors.

Most important of all, it was warm and cozy—there were radiators throughout the school. On an October day in Albania, especially if it was raining, we would be bundled up in our heavy coats and shiv-ering. In the winter, our feet and legs got numb from the cold, and we had to stand up and move around from time to time. It was never warm enough.

Outside the main office, a middle-aged woman approached us. "Hello, hello, ladies. You two must be the twins we were talking about." She wore no makeup and her hair was short, giving her a boyish appearance.

Don Carlos nodded and smiled. "Oh, yes. These are the new students."

"You must be Don Carlos, and you must be their father." She turned to Dad. "It's very nice to meet you. I'm Mrs. Brown, the head of the English department." She shook hands with the two men and then shook hands with Deti and me. "You are so identical—how do your parents tell you apart?"

"It isn't that hard," Deti said. "You'll get used to it."

Mrs. Brown studied our faces and then shook her head, grinning. "I'm not so sure about that."

We followed her down the hall, and she stopped at the room where the exam would take place. "It isn't too difficult, girls. You seem pretty fluent in English, so you probably won't have any trouble."

Still, I was nervous. Deti too. Like me, she was biting her lower lip.

Mrs. Brown held the door open for us. The room was large with long, thick purple curtains that gave the air a serious, but secure feeling.

"Good luck, girls," Don Carlos said, smiling at us. "I gave your dad a map so he could walk you back to the hotel after the test."

"Thank you, Don Carlos!" This wonderful man had helped us in so many ways.

Mrs. Brown said to Dad, "Mr. Zalli, you can wait in the office if you wish. The test will take about forty-five minutes."

After translating to Dad, I joined Deti in giving him a kiss, and then we entered the room. Mrs. Brown removed two papers from a folder she was carrying, gave one to each of us, and directed us to desks five rows apart.

Deti's face fell. She was definitely not happy about being separated from her twin for the first time at school. I knew her inside out, perhaps even better than she knew herself—every single fear, doubt, and insecurity. Being near me gave her the comfort that nobody and nothing else could offer. She followed every step I took. That was how much she trusted me. I was Deti, and Deti was me.

"Yes, you can do it, my cute puppy," I told her in Albanian.

She winked, her way of reassuring me she was fine.

"Ready, girls?" Mrs. Brown said.

"Yes!"

"Go ahead and begin. I'll stay here with you." Sitting at the front desk, she picked up a book and started to read.

The test was easier than we expected. Our work with Mrs. Alma, our English teacher in Albania, had paid off. The minutes passed quickly, and when Mrs. Brown told us to put our pens down, we had already finished. In fact we'd had time to double-check our answers.

"So how was it?" she asked.

"Not too bad," Deti said, looking relieved.

"Brilliant. We might have two new students in the school then. Our first twins, aye? If you wait a couple of minutes, I'll go to the headmaster's office and tell him you're here. He would like to meet you both."

As soon as she left, Deti said, as I knew she would, "Gita, you go first and talk to him. Please. You have to lead the way. You know me. I'm shyer than you, and we have to look confident in front of him."

Sometimes it was annoying that Deti made me take the first step, to be in charge. I was shy too, but if I didn't do what she wanted, she would find another way to force me.

Like the time when we were eight years old. It was Sunday and we went to meet Dad at his office at Albpetrol. He had given permission to an American group to use the auditorium to spread the word of Jesus Christ among the kids.

When we arrived, we could hear kids singing songs. It was loud but sounded super cool. Dad knocked on the door and introduced Deti and me to the American group so we could also join in.

Inside were rows and rows of kids holding song books. They were so kind to welcome us with applause, but it was embarrassing to be the center of attention. We took seats on the side, somewhere in the middle of the large room. After a while it was game time. The American leader of the team picked three people to compete for a balloon game, and Deti was one of them. She was so shy she refused to stand up.

"Gita, you go," she hissed, giving me a pinch.

"No." I didn't move.

"Please."

Everyone was watching us now.

Deti yanked me out of the chair and gave me a push. Furious with my sister and more embarrassed than ever, I stood in front of all the kids and tried to blow up the balloon faster than my two competitors.

I came in last. Why did Deti do this to me? Yet I understood how uneasy and fearful she could be with people she didn't know. After the game, I was no longer angry with her.

Now again at the Channel School, I had no choice. Since I was the stronger twin, Deti needed me to talk to the headmaster first.

Mrs. Brown poked her head into the room. "Okay, girls. Mr. Fox is waiting for you."

We followed her down the long, empty corridor and came to a white door. Taped at eye level was a hand-drawn picture of a fox, and underneath, it read, "Come on in. I don't bite." With a funny cartoon greeting like that, the headmaster had to be a nice guy.

A blue-eyed boy appeared behind us. "Mrs. Brown, can I have a chat with you?"

"Wayne, what are you doing here?" she said sternly. "Shouldn't you be in class?"

"I was just waiting to talk to you. I was in your office but you weren't there," the boy said in a whiny voice.

Wow! Was that the way the students talked to their teachers?

Mrs. Brown looked at Deti and me. "Are you going to be all right? Just knock on the door."

"Of course."

When the student and Mrs. Brown were out of ear shot, Deti said, "Go ahead."

Sure, I was the one who would have to do this. I took a deep breath and gently tapped on the door.

"Come on in. I don't bite," a man's voice called out.

Deti giggled.

I kicked her foot. "Be quiet, will you?" I stifled a laugh and frowned at her. We couldn't look like idiots. We had to make a good impression.

Just then, Mr. Fox opened the door. "Come on in. I don't bite."

At once all the laughter and game playing vanished, and my legs started to tremble. Before us stood a tall fiftyish man with a few patches of hair on top of an otherwise bald head.

"Gosh, am I seeing double?" he said. "So you must be the Zalli twins. Please take a seat, girls."

We sat on the comfy black chairs across from Mr. Fox's desk. He glanced back and forth at us. "How do people tell you apart? No, let me guess who you are first." Cupping his chin in his hand, he studied each of us and then pointed at me. "You must be Detina."

Deti giggled. "No, she's Gita. We're used to people mixing us up. It happens all the time."

"I bet one day I'll be able to do it." When he smiled, his whole face lit up.

Deti's shyness vanished. Mr. Fox was so easy to talk to, so friendly, definitely not scary like Mrs. Nat or Mrs. Ramina back in Albania. Maybe he could see from our expressions that we were hard workers—or was he just a fan of twins? It really didn't matter. We were talking and laughing with an English headmaster!

CHAPTER 21

Where the Hell Is Albania?

Deti

October 18, 1999

As the four of us walked into the hotel lobby carrying groceries, a beaming Don Carlos greeted us. "Girls, Mrs. Brown just called. You passed the test. Congratulations! You are now the two newest students at the Channel School."

Did he really say what I thought he said? I was almost afraid to believe him. "You mean . . . it's a done deal?"

He laughed. "Yes, yes, it's a done deal."

Both Mom and Dad cried tears of joy. This was the first time in the past three months that I'd seen them really happy. Our dream was becoming a reality. Their precious daughters were now enrolled in an English school.

Think of it.

We hugged each other again and again. I grabbed Gita's hands and we twirled around the room, our hair flying out behind us.

"And now you must think about buying the school uniform," Don Carlos said. "And school shoes too."

Our first English clothes!

I pulled Gita to me in another hug. "We did it," I whispered.

"Of course we did," she whispered back, hugging me even tighter.

❧

October 25, 1999

Our first day of English school. I couldn't have slept more than a couple of minutes. Full of nerves, but oh so excited. I loved my school uniform, the white shirt, dark red top, and gray trousers. I could see myself in Gita. She looked pretty. The whole outfit fit her well. Since I was her sosie, it must have suited me too.

We were nearly ready to go—but not quite. Mom was having problems with the tie. After trying ten times, she still couldn't get it right. I started to panic. We couldn't be late for school on our first day—but then, we didn't want to break any school uniform rules either.

Gita raced downstairs to see if Don Carlos could help. I was right behind her. Surely he could do it.

"I would be glad to tie them for you," he said. "You are like my granddaughters. Come here." He set to work on Gita's tie first.

I watched carefully to learn, but his fingers moved like a magician's, too quick for me to follow. When he was done, Gita looked so sharp and grown-up.

My turn now. If it looked good on Gita, it would look good on me, and it did. But now I really panicked. If we walked to school, we'd be late. I was too embarrassed to ask Don Carlos to give us a lift—the school was only fifteen minutes away by car. Gita wouldn't ask him either, even though I kicked her foot, demanding that she ask him. Maybe I needed to be stronger so I could do the asking instead of depending on my sister or someone else—but I couldn't help it.

Don Carlos must have gotten the message anyway. He glanced at his watch. "You girls can't be late on your first day. I'll give you a ride."

"Oh, thank you, Don Carlos." I smiled broadly at him. Dad came with us too.

Mr. Fox was waiting for us outside his office. "Good morning! I would like to introduce you to two girls who will be your classmates. Harper and Dawn, this is Argita and Detina. They will tell you which one is which."

The girls couldn't have looked more different. Harper had brown eyes and short, curly brown hair, and Dawn had blue eyes and long, straight blond hair. But both girls were almost a head taller than Gita and me. It was hard to believe they were thirteen and our classmates. I couldn't take my eyes off their faces. Their skin was so clear. No pimples, and both girls were wearing blue eye shadow.

Back in Albania, Gita and I were the second tallest in the class, everyone had pimples, and only grown-ups wore makeup.

"Harper and Dawn will take you to your classrooms and guide you around the school for the first week," Mr. Fox said. He took off with Dad and Don Carlos, leaving us alone with the two girls.

"Where do you guys come from?" Harper asked. She had a hard, unpleasant voice.

"Albania," Gita said cheerfully.

Harper exchanged a surprised look with Dawn and let out a short, forced laugh. Nervously I squeezed Gita's hand.

"Where the hell is Albania?" Harper asked.

"Sorry?" Gita pretended not to understand.

"Wheerrre the hellll is Albania?" Harper asked slowly, drawing out each letter in a nasty way. This time it was impossible not to understand her. I squeezed Gita's hand again. She needed to answer.

"It's close to Greece and Italy," she said coolly.

Harper narrowed her eyes. "Albania is like Slovakia, isn't it?"

"Gosh, I don't think I'd like to go there," Dawn said.

Gita didn't respond. What else was there to say? She was offended and so was I. This was our first chat with two of our English classmates. Now both girls were laughing. What was so funny?

Without saying another word to us, Harper and Dawn turned and started walking down the hallway. We didn't know where to go, so we had to follow them. Gita smiled bravely at me, pretending not to be upset. Maybe she didn't want to worry me.

The girls stopped outside a classroom where several other students milled around talking and joking. Two of the guys stood out because of their red hair. I'd never seen hair that color before. Did they dye it?

England was an advanced country—red hair could be a fashion thing. I couldn't help staring at them.

Harper and Dawn mingled with the other girls, and since they were supposed to be our guides, we stayed close by. Like them, the other girls wore makeup and looked much older than our classmates in Albania.

Ignoring us, Harper and Dawn formed a tight circle with four other girls. Awkwardly Gita and I stood behind them, excited, curious, and shy. Maybe in a minute or so, they would introduce us to the others.

But nothing happened. Seconds ticked by, then minutes, and the girls kept chattering among themselves. It was important for us to make a good first impression, but that wouldn't be a problem—we had always gotten along well with our school friends.

Five minutes passed and we were still waiting to be introduced. Then another five minutes went by and still nothing. Gita's face, so bright with joy when we had first arrived at school, now looked sad and worried. Like mine, I was sure.

"You have to go say hello," I whispered to her in Albanian.

She nodded. No fight, no resistance. We had the same thoughts. There was no choice. We had to break into that circle and introduce ourselves. This was all new and scary. We weren't used to being on the outside. I was right behind Gita. As soon as she broke through, I knew she would make room for me too.

Gita ducked her head into the circle. "Hi, I'm Argita."

"Sorry?" A blue-eyed brunette with long straight hair stared blankly at her.

"I'm Argita."

The brunette turned to Harper, her eyebrows darting upward like two arrows. "Who the hell is she?"

"*They.* Who the hell are *they,*" Harper sneered, her eyes flashing with disgust.

"What?" the brunette asked.

"It's two of them. They're twins."

"What are they doing here?"

"They're the new students."

"Where are they from?" an overweight blond asked. She had purple nail polish and matching purple lipstick.

"Albania," Harper said.

"Where the hell is Albania? Never heard of it."

"They say it's close to Greece and Italy, but I reckon it's close to Slovakia too."

"Are they refugees?" the blue-eyed brunette asked.

Harper eyed us directly. "Are you refugees?"

"Yes," Gita said in a small voice.

"Scums, go back to your own country," a small skinny girl said, her slanty green eyes full of hate.

Gita took my hand and led me away from the circle. What did "scum" mean? It definitely wasn't good. The girls talked among themselves, glancing over at us, not trying to hide that we were the subject of their conversation.

"What did we do?" I asked Gita. "Did we say something we shouldn't have?"

"I don't know."

I felt sick to my stomach. "They don't seem to want to be friends with us. What are we going to do? We need them to show us where to go."

Gita shook her head and said nothing.

So this was what rejection felt like. I missed my old school and my old friends. Who would have thought that I'd ever want to go back to a school with broken stairs and windows and wooden stools that made my bottom hurt so much?

How could I miss Albania, after all we'd been through? Well, I missed a part of it. I missed the familiar warmth that filled me with love and the security that came with it—and the sense of bonding that was so much a part of belonging.

Whatever confidence I'd had vanished. At least in Albania I was accepted for who I was. In this place, all of me was a foreigner.

"This isn't going to be easy," I said.

"You're still lucky."

"What do you mean?"

"You're not alone. You have me." She gave me a half smile.

Of course, she was right. I shouldn't be afraid. My sister would protect me, as she always had.

A chubby girl with glasses whose name we later learned was Chloe called over to us. "Come on, girls. Our French lesson starts in a few minutes."

We were the last to enter the classroom. I never let go of Gita's hand. She positioned herself at the front of the room next to the whiteboard so the teacher would notice her. We had gotten the message. We would have to introduce ourselves. Nobody else was going to do it for us.

The French teacher, a slim woman with a warm smile, came over to us. We soon discovered that there was seldom a time when she wasn't smiling.

"Hello, girls, I'm Mrs. Anna. It's so nice to meet you. Where do you come from?"

"Italy," I said.

"Albania," Gita said at the same time.

I glared at her. She blushed, making it even more obvious that one of us had lied. How humiliating. She had just ruined my reputation in front of the French teacher and the other thirty kids. If Gita had been clever, she wouldn't have told the teacher and the class the truth. The girls already didn't like us because they didn't like Albania—they didn't even know where it was. But English people liked Italy and Italians.

Mrs. Anna rephrased the question. "Do you come from Albania or Italy?" This wasn't a difficult question. We needed to answer it immediately.

"I've got this," I whispered to Gita in Albanian.

"We come from Albania, but since many people don't know where that is, we say Italy because it's better known. Albania is located very close to the south of Italy." The perfect response. And it all came so easily.

"So do you speak Italian?" Mrs. Anna asked.

"Yes, we do."

Mrs. Anna spoke to us briefly in Italian. What a surprise. She said she was impressed with our accent. "What about French? Do you speak any at all?"

"No, we've never studied it," Gita said.

"Don't worry, girls, I'll help you. The students here have been studying it for two years, but you'll catch up. Please take a seat."

We sat at two desks in the front, the third and fourth rows from the right. No one came over to introduce themselves. Worse, they were laughing at us from around the room. They saw us with different eyes, as if we were bugs or some other disgusting creature. Why? We wore the same school uniform. We were just like them. It was so strange—so heartbreaking.

Only a few minutes of the first class had passed, and I couldn't wait to go home. Gita said I was lucky because I wasn't alone, but that didn't help. Sadness was spilling from my soul. It was spilling from hers too, though she was pretending to hide it.

Fifty-five minutes later, the bell rang. The classes lasted ten minutes longer than they did in Albania and they were noisier. Students talked and laughed during the lesson. Mrs. Anna had to shout over them several times to be heard. It was hard for her to keep any kind of order. In Albania noisy behavior would be considered serious disrespect. Here everything was much less strict, and Mrs. Anna appeared to be softer than our teachers in Albania.

The students raced out of the classroom as if they were happy to escape "the French territory." But where did we go next?

We were about to leave and follow our "helpful" guides when Mrs. Anna called over to us. "Did you girls understand anything during the lesson?" Without waiting for an answer, she smiled and said, "I'd be happy to help you during lunchtime so you can catch up with the rest of the group."

What a kind offer. Besides Mr. Fox, Mrs. Anna was the only other nice person we'd talked to that day.

"Thank you, we would like that," Gita said.

Harper and Dawn disappeared out the door as Mrs. Anna chattered on and we tried to focus on what she was saying. We couldn't lose our guides!

Finally, we were able to excuse ourselves. We rushed into the hall, but the two girls were nowhere.

"Now what?" I looked at Gita and she looked at me. We stood alone. Everyone else had gone to their next classroom.

"I heard some students say we had math," Gita said.

"So that's the classroom we have to find." This was certainly not the kind of welcome we'd expected. My eyes brimmed with tears. Two drops rolled down my cheeks.

"Stop it! Don't be negative," Gita scolded.

I wiped my eyes with the back of my hand. Together we trudged down the empty hallway. All the classroom doors were closed. The lessons had started, and we still didn't know where to go. We were lost in this weird world where none of the students wanted to acknowledge our existence.

Gita peered through the window of the classroom at the end of the hall, searching for two students who resembled Harper and Dawn. It was hard to remember the faces of the other students. At least those two girls' faces were somewhat familiar.

"I don't recognize anyone in that room," she said.

"Let's go back and check the room next to the French class," I said.

Never had this happened to us before. Ever.

A door near the French classroom opened, and Mrs. Anna reappeared. "Girls, are you all right?" She eyed us anxiously.

"We're lost, actually," Gita said. "Can you please tell us where our math class is?"

More tears ran down my face. Gita jerked my hand, signaling to me to stop crying.

Mrs. Anna saw the tears. "Of course," she said softly. "Follow me."

Our footsteps echoed loudly on the stairway. Gita's face was pale and drawn, just as mine must have been.

Mrs. Anna smiled brightly as we arrived at one of the classroom doors. "Here you go. But before I leave, you have to give me a smile. Chop! Chop! You've got to do it quick. After all, we don't want the math teacher to see you sad."

At once both of us gave Mrs. Anna a broad smile and watched her as she continued down the corridor. But our smiles faded when we looked through the window and saw that the teacher had already started the lesson. A couple of rows back, Harper was whispering in Dawn's ear.

Several minutes passed, and we were still holding each other's hands outside the classroom. I was depending on Gita, but she couldn't get herself to open the door.

We heard steps approaching. Mrs. Anna again. "You still haven't gone in? C'mon, let me introduce you to Mr. Andy."

She knocked and when he opened the door, she said, "Mr. Andy, I'm sorry to interrupt you. I want to introduce you to the two new students. As you can tell, they're twins. She could be Detina"—motioning toward me—"and she could be Argita"—motioning toward Gita. "Is that right, girls?"

"You got it right, miss," I said.

"Well let's pretend I got it right even if I didn't. Please give me the satisfaction this one time."

Mr. Andy was tall and slim, maybe in his early forties, with thinning hair. Although he was dressed smartly in a white button-down shirt and brown trousers, I was surprised to see that his shoes were badly worn. How could a teacher come to work like that? Back in Albania, everyone thought the British people were rich. Maybe this wasn't entirely true.

He glanced back and forth at us, as most people do when they first meet us. "I was expecting you, but—" He paused. "What I wasn't expecting is for you to be identical." He bent forward to look at us more closely. "You know, girls, my brother and I are twins too, but people have always been able to tell us apart. Although we have tricked them sometimes." He winked at us. "But you wouldn't do that, would you?"

"Well, it depends on the circumstances," I said, cheekily winking back at him.

"Oh, really?" He grinned. "That means I don't have much time to waste. I should get going and spot the difference as soon as possible."

"It's their first day of school in England," Mrs. Anna said. "They come from Albania. Please make sure they both feel comfortable." Her voice was so soft and sweet. She really cared about us.

"Absolutely, Mrs. Anna. Not to worry about that." Mr. Andy nodded reassuringly. "Thanks ever so much for all your help."

After she left, Mr. Andy surveyed the classroom and pointed to two empty desks. "Could you please sit in the second row, girls? I'll get you your exercise books."

He opened a drawer in his desk, removed two pairs of red and blue notebooks, and brought them over to us. "The red books are for class and the blue ones are for homework. Now, please turn to page 156 and work on the exercises. How good are you in math?"

"We're good," Gita said.

"How many minutes do we have?" I asked him, ready to race with myself.

"You have thirty minutes. I don't expect you to finish all the exercises by then. I don't think anyone will manage to do that anyway, but don't get me wrong—try your best and do as much as you can in the time that's left."

Forgetting about Harper and Dawn, I focused on the exercises. I read the first one carefully, and to my delight, I discovered I understood it completely. I raced with Gita just as I always did in Albania. The next exercise was also easy, and so were the rest. I looked at the large round black clock mounted in the corner of the classroom. Fifteen minutes since I started working on the exercises and I was finished. Thirty seconds later, Gita also put down her pencil. She shook her head, smiling because she hadn't beat my time.

We stayed seated, silently agreeing that we wouldn't tell Mr. Andy we had finished. The last thing we wanted to do was become the center of attention again. We needed to keep our mouths shut. It would help us hide.

But when I glanced over at Mr. Andy, I saw him watching us, a concerned look on his face. He approached and crouched down by our desks. "Do you understand the exercises, girls?" he whispered. "Do you need some help? I know it must be difficult for you, given that English isn't your native language."

"We finished, sir."

His eyebrows shot up. "You *finished?* Can I see what you've done?"

"Sure," we both said.

He picked up our notebooks and studied our answers. Anxiously I waited for him to finish, hoping he wouldn't find any mistakes.

"Very impressive indeed." At length he handed our books back to us. "That's excellent."

His words cut through the silence in the classroom, followed by a pencil clattering to the floor. It belonged to a red-haired boy openly staring at us. He gaped first at me, then at Gita, then back at me again. Several more heads bobbed up and looked at us. Mr. Andy checked the clock, as if he didn't believe how little time had gone by. We finished every exercise on that page within sixteen minutes.

The whispering around us grew louder. Now all the students were looking at us. Two guys in the back were talking to each other.

"How could they be finished?"

"I haven't even gotten through the first exercise. Do you believe them?"

A wave of confusion swept over me. Had we done something wrong? The tallest boy in the classroom shot daggers at us. "Did they really finish all the exercises, sir?" he asked. "That's impossible!"

My heart skipped a beat. As much as I wanted to speak up, I simply couldn't.

Mr. Andy came to our rescue. "Thank you for your concern, Anthony, but my advice is not to worry about them. You focus on yourself. And if you really want to know, they not only finished the exercises but did them all correctly."

"Mr. Andy, are you positive that you checked their answers against the right page in your book? Sometimes in the past, you know, you've checked our answers against the wrong page."

What did Anthony just say? Was he contradicting the teacher? Teasing him? How could he be so disrespectful? This would never happen in Albania, or if it did, the punishment would be severe.

Mr. Andy's face turned bright red. The whole class was laughing.

Later we learned that Anthony was one of the most popular guys in the school and considered the top math student. What a shock to have two foreign girls swoop into the classroom and invade his space!

CHAPTER 22

"Do Not Fight!"

Gita

November 1, 1999

After the first week, the English school didn't seem so strange. We got much better at finding our classrooms and now carried a class schedule so we didn't have to depend on Harper and Dawn.

History was by far my favorite class, unlike anything we'd ever had in Albania. The teacher, Mr. Evan, gray-haired with small dark eyes, always wore a sharp tailored suit and delivered polished, well-prepared lessons. In some ways, he reminded me of President Bill Clinton.

When Mr. Evan talked about World War II and the aerial combats that took place between the Brits and Germans during the fall of 1940, he came alive, his voice booming. But he didn't just talk. He showed us movies. After everyone was seated, he closed the curtains, turned off the lights, and flipped on the huge TV screen at the front of the class.

Deti and I had never gone to a movie before, but we were sure it was similar to Mr. Evan's "theater." Every so often he paused the video and, with a thin white stick, pointed out certain details on the screen. I would never have dreamed of watching a movie and getting a history lesson at the same time. All of us were spellbound—no slackers or sleepers in his class. We could actually watch historical events unfolding in front of us.

Back in Albania, Mrs. Linda's classes consisted only of words, thousands and thousands of them stubbornly lodged in a book. Page after page of lifeless facts that we had to memorize.

One time Mrs. Linda asked Deti and me to make thirty photocopies of the test questions. She had singled us out not just because we were straight A students, but also because Albpetrol, where Dad worked, had fancy photocopying machines. Copy machines were scarce, and the school certainly didn't have any.

We kept a copy of the questions, of course—but we were equal opportunists. It seemed hardly fair to keep this valuable information to ourselves. Deti went to Lefta's house and called five of our friends so we could discuss the test answers. On Saturday afternoon before the text on Monday, we all gathered at our friend Vera's house. We worked into the evening, going through each of the test questions. But none of us could answer more than one of them, even with an open book.

Mr. Evan's lessons were so much better. I didn't understand all the English words he used, but I could easily remember the main facts. He was also our homeroom teacher. Every morning we reported first to his classroom, where he took attendance with a posh electronic device that beeped whenever he entered a name.

In Albania each teacher took attendance at the start of their lesson. When our name was called, we stood up and shouted "Present!" and the teachers would put a check by our name. Mr. Evan didn't need to do that. With his device, he completed the roll by himself by looking around and checking to see who was there.

Deti and I were starting to remember people's faces and names, now recognizing most of the students in our classes. In homeroom, and in many of our other classes, we sat next to Sophia. Of all the students, she was the only one who ever smiled at us. She even complimented us that first day in math class. "Well done! You girls beat Anthony. Nobody's ever done that before."

Sophia was more like us and our friends in Albania. She wore glasses and no makeup, and her natural brown hair was frizzy and a bit dull. The other girls had smooth, shiny hair. At first I was puzzled by this. What made their hair so shiny and smooth? Was it their diet or the shampoo they used to wash their hair? When I asked Sophia what she thought was wrong with our hair, she said, "Nothing.

It's natural. The other girls' hair looks different because they either straighten it or dye it."

What a relief to learn that we weren't different from the other girls after all. But that wasn't what they thought. It was obvious how they felt about us. They knew we were from Albania, and since they had a vague idea that it was somewhere near Czechoslovakia and Hungary, they called us Slovaks. To them, in their England, all Slovaks were outcasts, intruders.

Although many actual Slovakian girls attended the Channel School, they were in a grade or two ahead of us. One of the girls, Valentina, who must have been fifteen, had a sweet, gentle face and manner. She wore makeup like the English girls, and judging from her brown eyebrows, I assumed her long, straight black hair wasn't her natural color. Standing tall and elegant, she made me think of Pocahontas.

Nothing was wrong with Valentina, apart from being more beautiful than any of the English girls I'd met so far. Still, the students didn't like her. "Get out of here, Slovak!" they would say. Valentina lowered her head and turned quickly away from them.

Their words cut through me. We had already had a taste of that treatment ourselves. Deti and I were "foreigners" like Valentina. Our classmates had no intention of accepting us. They either hurled hostile remarks at us or deliberately excluded us from their conversations. The bitter truth was sinking in.

November 17, 1999

Today we would go to the cafeteria for the first time. We had been packing lunch bags at home, but we didn't have to do that anymore. As refugees in England, we were eligible for school lunches paid by Social Services. They cost a pound and half each. The short-haired woman at the cash register gave us a green card, allowing us to order a main meal and even a dessert.

In the cafeteria, we took our place in the long line. A boy at the front had just placed his meal on one of the blue trays. Standing on my tiptoes, I peered over the heads of the others to see what was on his plate. Something I'd never seen before, but I wanted to try it. Deti too. "How can we tell the server what we want if we don't know what it is?" I asked her nervously.

"It's okay," she said. "Point to it like Camilla does."

She was right. Camilla, the waitress at the hotel, got along very well with her broken English.

"That's easy for you to say," I said.

Deti was so cheeky. I was in front of her, so when it was our turn to order, I would have to be the one to speak up. She planned it that way. When the server asked her what she wanted, all she had to say was, "The same."

We moved up in line, and now only four students were in front of us. If I bent to the side, I could get a full view of all the different meals. Everything looked so interesting, and the steam rising from the heated dishes filled the air with tangy aromas. Ooh, I was so hungry! I couldn't wait to eat.

Deti tapped on my shoulder and smiled. If only she would be willing to do the ordering and not make me do it. Just then I turned and saw a group of girls heading toward us. From their brisk, determined stride and angry faces, I knew we were in trouble. Instantly, my heart started pounding. Shakily I said to Deti, "Whatever happens, do *not* fight."

"What are you talking about?"

"Quick—look to your left."

It was too late. The five girls closed in around us fast, pulling us out of line. No doubt, they could tell how scared I was, but I couldn't help it. Every part of me was shaking.

Kim, a short, chubby redhead, stepped closer. "Why the fuck are you invading our canteen?" The four other girls stood on either side of her, their arms crossed in front of them, waiting for an explanation.

"We're going to have some lunch" Deti said calmly.

"We don't think so," Shannon said, her eyes cold and accusing, as if we were criminals who had stolen something of hers.

I placed my hand on Deti's back and tapped it lightly, warning her to ignore them and not get involved in a fight. I could feel the anger already boiling up inside her. We moved back into the line, closer to the serving counter.

"Hey, we're talking to you!" Kim raised her voice as Shannon planted herself directly in front of me and raised a fist, ready to punch me in the face.

Desperately I begged the woman at the cash register to help us. She looked up at me and then at the girls, but said nothing.

Shannon raised both fists now. "Get the fuck out of here or I'll break your fucking teeth." She moved closer and shoved one of her fists in my face and the other in Deti's. I flinched, too shocked or scared or embarrassed to find my voice. Some of the kids in line were laughing at us, enjoying the little scene.

Kim snatched the green card from my hand and passed it to the other three girls. Numbly I watched them tear it into tiny pieces. I controlled my anger, but Deti wouldn't keep her cool much longer. *Oh Deti, please, please, don't say anything, don't do anything. It would be such a mistake.*

I wanted to cry, but I wouldn't give them the satisfaction. For the first time in my life, I was waiting to get beaten up by my schoolmates. My mind raced. I would do whatever I could to cover my face so at least I wouldn't have any bruises.

"Hey, what is happening here?" A woman called out.

The girls spun around as the woman approached. It was Mrs. Brown.

"Nothing. We came to say hi to the girls," Shannon said, her voice suddenly dripping with innocence.

"That's not the impression I got," Mrs. Brown said. She eyed Shannon suspiciously.

"We swear," Kim said. "We're just curious to find out more about the twins."

"Hmm." Mrs. Brown wasn't buying it. "Detina and Argita, is that true?"

I squeezed Deti's hand so she wouldn't answer. Telling the truth might backfire on us. We saw Mrs. Brown twice a week in English class, but we saw the girls every day. What they didn't do to us today they might do to us tomorrow, twice as bad. And then what?

Mrs. Brown fastened her eyes on Shannon and Kim. "Listen to me very carefully, all of you." She looked at each of the five girls separately. "If I find out that you have been bullying the twins, you will all be in trouble. Is that clear?"

Our savior. Sullenly the girls lowered their heads and said nothing. There was nothing to say.

Mrs. Brown waved her hand at them. "Now go away."

The girls vanished through the canteen door. Mrs. Brown turned to us, her eyes now soft and kind. "Please, girls, if anyone treats you badly, let me know and I will deal with it. It's going to get better, I promise." She lightly touched Deti's shoulder.

Part of me was pleased that Mrs. Brown was on our side, but I was also well aware that a teacher, even Mrs. Brown, could only do so much.

I slowly stopped shaking. This wasn't the end of our trouble—in fact it was probably only the beginning.

Deti and I weren't hungry anymore.

November 30, 1999

From the moment I arrived at school, I began to count the hours until it was time to go home.

It was like the two of us had been sucked into a dark underworld, lurking with unpredictable dangers. Every day the tension built a little bit more. When would the bullies strike again and what could we do to keep it from happening? Nothing. There was nothing to do but wait.

As I passed through the halls from one classroom to the next, I felt like I had weights on my feet and couldn't walk fast enough to escape the Terrible Something following me or trying to trip me up. I could never relax. The best part of every school day was when the final bell rang.

How different from Albania. I had always loved school, but not anymore. Gone was my usual upbeat spirit. Here in England, that spirit had abandoned me. What a coward it was. It hid from me during the entire school day, leaving me with an empty wasted feeling. When I got like this, weak and powerless, I couldn't protect myself, so I was no use to Deti either.

Then at three-thirty, as soon as I was on the other side of the school's large iron gate, all my sad thoughts vanished. I clasped Deti's hand, and joyfully we walked home—free! We breathed the fresh air and looked up at the wide-open sky protecting us. No fear. Today we were lucky. Three hours had gone by without any of the kids badgering us with names, which we had discovered really did hurt just as much as sticks and stones.

The words grated on my ears: "We hate you, Slovaks. Go back to your country!"

What did we do to be treated like such scum? And we weren't even Slovaks, but if we were, what did these kids have against them? Their hatred must have come from family conversations. They must have heard racist talk from their parents and other adults.

How were we different? Weren't we all human beings? Didn't we all have wishes, hopes, and dreams—and the same craving to be liked and accepted for who we were?

Today we might have escaped, but tomorrow it would be the same thing all over again. Once more they would come after us. *Don't go there. Enjoy today. Enjoy this moment.*

Our walk from school to the Gran Canaria Hotel took thirty-five minutes. On our way home, we talked only of Albania and our cousins Frida and Lela, our grandparents, and our friends. We had been away for only four months, yet we missed them so much.

Deti told me jokes and made me laugh, making sure I was happy before we got home. We didn't want Mom and Dad to have even the slightest clue about what was going on at school. They were worried enough, with all the stress about Home Office papers, the debt, and the hardship of our English immigration.

Our parents waited at the main entrance of the hotel to welcome us with a hug and a kiss. "How was school today?"

They asked all the predictable questions, and my answers, filled with superlatives, tarnished the meaning of those beautiful words: "Super, great, brilliant, exciting. We love it . . ." It was getting harder and harder to keep pretending. How long could I put up a front? Mom wanted to know every detail, and all I wanted to do was forget until the next day.

Deti's mask of deception never cracked. How did she do that? No sadness, bitterness, or fear—nothing except delight: she'd had a fantastic day at school. She went on to tell them that even though her classmates hadn't known her for very long and her English wasn't perfect yet, they all liked her and respected her tremendously. They respected me too, she said, smiling confidently, because I was her sister.

Yes, Deti had to be the heroine, the strongest girl in the class. Her happiness was so real and alive I almost believed it was true. But then a few hours later, I found her alone in the bathroom, sobbing.

"I wish Frida and Lela were here," she whispered, lifting her tear-streaked face. Her nose was red and runny, and her cheeks were splotchy from crying. Feeling her desperation, I started tearing up myself. We locked the door of the tiny bathroom and stayed there until our eyes were no longer red and we had completely recovered. Mom and Dad must never see us like this.

Nothing happened over the next couple of days, but Deti and I stayed on our guard, prepared for the worst. A week passed. Then on Tuesday, December 7, as we set out for home, I sensed that we were being followed. Cautiously I turned my head around and glanced over my shoulder.

It was those girls, the mean ones, and some of the boys. They were following us all right. A cold shudder passed through me.

Deti caught sight of them too. I clasped her hand tightly and the two of us quickened our pace. We had to stay together.

They drew closer, swearing at us, but we ignored them, pretending not to understand. Several more minutes passed. We were nearly at home. They would follow us all the way because they wanted to see where we lived. They had a vicious plan for us.

We were about half a block from the hotel. Mom and Dad waited at the entrance, but they hadn't caught sight of us yet. "Keep walking," I said.

Ignoring Mom and Dad, we went past the hotel. The bullies would never find our home. I pulled Deti's hand and changed our route, going around in circles.

I prayed that other people would be on the street with us. Then if the bullies attacked, we could ask for help.

Two hours later, exhausted, we finally lost them. It was safe to go home. Mom would surely interrogate us now, and we would have no choice but to tell the truth. She and Dad needed to know. We couldn't pretend any longer.

Deti

December 16, 1999

Today at the end of the school day, Dad waited for us at the iron gate to walk us home. Now that he met us after school, nine days had passed by without any incidents.

Maybe Mrs. Brown was right, maybe it would get better with time. We greeted Dad with big hugs, and the three of us set out for home, Gita and I chattering away, telling Dad everything that had happened at school today.

We turned the corner and I saw her. Several steps ahead of us, one of the girls who had bullied us constantly ever since we started school. Fair with a face full of freckles, she could turn ugly and mean in an instant. She had already changed out of her uniform and was walking her puppy. Stopping, she bent down and stroked the puppy with tenderness. How could that witch take such good care of a cute little dog? Could she be the same person?

I'd never forget what she did a couple of weeks before. Joined by three other girls, she marched up to Gita and me. "You stink," she spat out. "And you have hairy arms. You shouldn't be in our school." She was about to grab hold of Gita's hair and yank it, but Mrs. Jane, the librarian, who had been watching the girls accosting us, hurried over and sent them running.

That girl was a menace and I'd had enough. Alone now, she didn't have any of her friends to help defend her. I dropped my school bag and ran as fast as I could over to her, Gita right behind me, trying to catch up. "Deti, don't!"

When I reached the girl, she stood up and her eyes widened in fear. She knew what was coming. Gita waved her hands, begging me to stop, her hair flying around her.

I caught my breath and assumed a karate pre-fight position. It was now or never. I had to act quickly. Softly I kicked the girl's right leg, stepped forward, and then kicked her left leg. Losing her balance, she fell to the ground. The puppy started to bark furiously. Little did the blessed creature know what his cruel owner had done to Gita and me.

"Leave me alone!" the girl cried out weakly.

"Call us names again and I'll break your neck. Do you understand?" I yelled.

The girl bobbed her head up and down like the victim she was not.

"What the hell are you doing?" Gita asked me in Albanian, grabbing hold of my arm. "Are you satisfied? Did you win the trophy?"

At once she made me see what I had done. I didn't feel satisfied or like a winner. "I only threw two punches in the air to scare her." I wished I felt as confident as I sounded. Only a minute ago, I was convinced about hitting her so hard she would never forget it.

"What do you think will happen tomorrow at school when she

comes over with her friends to fight us? You idiot, I can't let you get away from me for a minute."

"Come here, immediately!" Dad shouted.

The girl got to her feet and scrambled off with her dog.

When Gita and I reached Dad, I said, "I've done nothing wrong. I just scared her so she wouldn't bother us again. It's okay. I'm done with her, Dad."

"No, it is not okay!" Dad had such a fierce expression on his face, I was afraid to look into his eyes. "What do you think you're doing? Is that what I have been teaching you all these years?"

I bowed my head, feeling ashamed and trying to console myself. At least I'd made use of some of Jean-Claude Van Damme's teaching lessons.

"Don't you dare fight with people again!"

"I promise," I said at once.

For a moment I wished Dad could understand me better. Did he think I enjoyed it? This was my first British fight, and it was nothing like I thought it would be. In fact, it almost felt as if I had fought with myself. My whole body was shaking. My legs felt weak. I let my frustration get the best of me. I exploded and now I was paying for it.

As we continued on to the hotel, Dad didn't say anything. I didn't dare say anything either.

Gita reached for my hand, already forgiving me. She read my heart. She knew why I did it. The bullying and racism at school had been too much for us. But I didn't want to fight anymore.

CHAPTER 23

Home: Albania or England?

Deti

December 23, 1999

Christmas vacation was almost here. Even if everything else was miserable compared to our former life in Albania, at least we had an English Christmas to look forward to.

In Albania, most people aren't affiliated with any particular religion so they don't celebrate the holidays. In history class, I learned that Albania was considered a Muslim country because it had been under Ottoman and Muslim rule for five centuries. But after World War II, the communist government outlawed religion and persecuted Christians and Muslims, forcing many Albanians to forsake their beliefs until the fall of communism in 1990.

Mom's family is Muslim, though they don't practice it, whereas Dad's family is Orthodox Christian. When Gita and I were young, Grandma Lira and Grandpa Llazi told us stories about Jesus and the saints and about the many miracles Jesus had worked throughout his life to help mankind. They had taught us to love him.

Every Christmas Eve in Albania, we would walk on the wide streets of Bubullimë with the rest of Dad's family to the beautiful Orthodox Church. Inside, we would light candles and pray to Jesus for the spirits of our loved ones who had died. We also prayed for our health and happiness and asked him to forgive our sins.

And then on Christmas morning, Mom would bake *shendetli*, a sherbet nut cake, and we'd bring it to our grandparents' home. Oh,

I missed the happy chatter of our wonderful family. They made me feel so safe, so loved.

I counted the days until Christmas, and finally it was only two days away. How I wished I could stop the clock so I could remain in this happy time of love and beauty, away from all the bullies at school.

Don Carlos had strung colored lights around the letters of the hotel sign and placed a large Christmas tree by the entrance. This was new to us, to see such a magnificent tree. He had decorated it with exquisite handmade ornaments and sparkling bulbs and draped it with strings of popcorn and hundreds of tiny colored lights. The silver icicles were the final touch—hundreds of them, completely covering the tree. At the very top was a beautiful white angel with a silver halo. I tried to jump up high enough to touch it, but Gita pulled me away, saying I had no right to touch things that didn't belong to me.

Beneath the tree was a hand-carved wooden crèche of the baby Jesus with Mother Mary, Father Joseph, and the Three Wise Men. And so many presents stacked up on either side—heaps and heaps of beautifully gift-wrapped packages of every shape and color. The pine needles smelled so fresh. Up and down the street, all the lamp posts were decorated with sprigs of holly and mistletoe. Across from us, the amusement park had a splendid display of dazzling lights that flashed on and off. So beautiful, they lit up my soul!

This seemed like a magical land where dreams surely came true. Everywhere, people were smiling and singing Christmas carols. We joined in, pretending we knew the words. Even Mom and Dad were smiling. Perhaps just for today, they could forget the bitter reality of our life here in England and celebrate the Christmas joy.

In the late afternoon on Christmas Eve, the four of us arrived at the ASDA store to shop for some Christmas food. "You can buy whatever you want," Mom said.

"But what about the money?" I said.

Dad put his arms around us. "Don't worry, we'll be fine."

What a treat! Gita and I ran around the store looking for delicious, inexpensive goodies. We spotted British milk chocolates and Italian amaretti cookies on the bottom shelf. And they cost only twenty-one pence. For a moment, we let our eyes wander to the other, much more expensive flavors on the top shelf, wrapped in fancy Christmas paper. No, not for us. Not when our parents were in debt. We were happy with what we had.

Mom and Dad filled the shopping cart with pasta, vegetables, rice, bread, tomatoes, olives, cheese, butter, eggs, flour, canned peach slices, Coke, Sprite, milk, and beer. Almost everything we bought was wrapped in blue-and-white packaging, the cheaper selections. As we checked out, the girl scanning our food stared at us. Who knew what she was thinking, but I didn't care. I wasn't embarrassed.

All that was missing was the turkey our grandparents used to raise for us so it would be ready for Christmas. That wasn't really a problem, since we bought many other wonderful items. Our bags were so heavy we could hardly carry them.

Outside it was dark already, and the temperature had dropped. A fierce wind had struck up, bringing with it an icy rain verging on sleet. It was a thirty-minute walk from the store to the hotel.

"Let's take a taxi, shall we?" Dad said.

"We can walk, Dad," I said at once. The fare was way too expensive.

"Yes, we'll be fine," Gita said. "We're not that far from home."

As we trudged along, we kept reassuring Dad that the bags weren't that heavy. But, oh, they really were heavy, and it was so cold. It would all be worth it, I kept telling myself.

Like soldiers we marched through the wind and rain, ignoring the icy needles on our bare faces, stopping every few minutes for a short rest. For the first time in five months, we would have real food. Did we care if it was inexpensive? Absolutely not. That day was special.

January 18, 2000

Our vacation ended far too soon, and Gita and I returned to school. Nothing had changed. The same bullying and racist taunts. How much longer could I hold off before letting go and hitting someone again?

Only Gita's eyes held me back.

Even on a day like today when we both got As on our chemistry test. During lunch period, we bundled up and went outside to the playground area to eat our sandwiches. Since the incident in the cafeteria, we stayed away from there.

Gita had just pulled her sandwich out of her lunch bag when a group of kids ganged up around us. "Slovaks, you shouldn't eat at our school," they yelled. "It's British property. Go back to your country where you belong!"

One of the kids stepped forward and gave Gita a hard shove. Her sandwich flew out of her hand and landed on the ground. I stared at the pieces of bread separated from the lunch meat, all dirty and disgusting, inedible. I was so angry at myself. It was my fault that they pushed Gita. How could I not have seen this coming?

Of the two of us, I was the one the kids hated the most. They called me the bad twin because I yelled back at them. Gita was the good twin. With her sweet smile and tremulous voice, she tried to pretend that none of this taunting really bothered her. Only I knew how much her heart pounded.

But this time was different. Angrily Gita slammed her lunch bag on the ground—I counted—one, two, three, four, five times. "I *will* get out of here!" she screamed. "I don't want to ever come back!"

Her words scared me. Then she started to weep.

I clutched her arm. "Gita, stop. Stop! They aren't worth it. They aren't worth your tears."

All the kids on the playground gathered close. Shrugging me off, Gita grabbed her school bag and ran toward the iron exit gate. She wasn't running away from school—she was running away from bullying and ignorance. She was giving up.

It was my turn to be strong and make her come back. I chased after her. "Gita, remember what you told me? You said, 'You're lucky because you have me.' Please stop running and listen to me." I caught up with her and hugged her tightly. All we had was each other in our small, sad world of suffering.

News spread fast. At least half the kids found out what had happened, along with Mr. Fox. He calmed Gita down and promised us that the bullies would pay for this. He already knew who they were, and he suspended them for three days. This wouldn't look good on their records, for sure.

For a short time afterward, the kids left us alone. But it didn't last.

April 17, 2000

Finally a piece of good news from Social Services. We were moving into a place of our own: an old three-story council house at 83 Earls Avenue in Folkestone, on the corner of the street. Only a hundred meters from the beach, and the largest place we had ever lived in.

It was furnished with an old-fashioned telephone, torn armchairs, a broken TV, and antique beds. The third-floor bedroom was small and cozy, the perfect refuge for Gita and me. Before we moved in, Mom bleached everything from top to bottom to get rid of the cigarette smoke and filth. She had Gita and me scrub the muddy blue carpet three times.

Now that the house was clean, it felt like we owned it, especially at night when Gita and I climbed the stairs to our refuge. We opened the sloped window and breathed in the fresh air. Then we counted the stars, wondering whether the same ones could be seen from Albania.

A few days after we moved in, Social Services came to see how we were doing and brought us some pans and utensils. Mom bought a frying pan to fry chips for us. It had been almost nine months since we had had them.

For so long, our lives had been filled with darkness and gloom, like the days in late autumn when it never seems to get light outside and the sky is blanketed with heavy gray clouds and the rain keeps coming down.

I prayed to God for some peace. School was hell and home was sad and tense. Our IND expired on January 31, 2000, almost three months before. A woman in Social Services told us that the Home Office would contact us soon.

Since the IND expiration, Dad hadn't slept much. We heard that the Home Office deported an Albanian family we had met recently. The British police came at two in the morning, woke them up, and took them to a refugee camp in Dover where they would stay until they were deported to Albania.

Any day now we were expecting the same thing.

The police made their calls at night when everyone was typically at home. If a family member wasn't there, the police couldn't deport any of them.

After I heard this, I started having nightmares. In one of them, the four of us were being held in a detention facility by the British police, who were about to hand us over to the Albanian Mafia to be imprisoned for life because we were illegal in England and owed them money we couldn't afford to pay back.

I woke with a start. Shivering, I looked at the clock. Three-fifteen. I clutched the bedcovers close, my hands cold and clammy. None of it was real. We were all safe, still in our house on Earls Avenue.

A glass of water would help me calm down. Softly I padded down the carpeted stairs to the kitchen. As I passed Mom and Dad's bedroom on the second floor, I noticed their door was half open. Maybe they had forgotten to close it.

I tiptoed into their room to make sure they were sleeping. That's when I saw Dad standing in the corner of the room by the window. He moved the curtains ever so slightly. Joining him, I peered outside and was blinded by the headlights of a car parked across the street. I jumped back. "What—?"

"Shhh!" He placed a finger over his mouth. He must have thought the vehicle was an unmarked police car. It had no lights on top.

Dad had already told us his plan if the police should come during the night. He would jump out of the bedroom window facing the garden and head to London to meet Uncle Dino, who was actually Mom's second cousin.

Gita and I had never met him. He had lived near our granddad's house in Laberia, a historic region in Southern Albania where the legendary Ali Pasha of Tepelena came from in the eighteenth century. The Labs were warlike, strong and fierce, and culturally different from the rest of the country. Mom told us to call him Uncle as a sign of respect.

When Uncle Berti heard that he had been living in London for almost two years, he contacted Uncle Dino's family in Albania for his phone number and gave it to Dad in case we needed help. Uncle Dino could be our savior on a night like this.

But the car drove off. It wasn't the police after all. We both breathed a sigh of relief.

Dad was our captain. He checked every car parked on the road. He was prepared to fight for us. Always.

CHAPTER 24

Breadwinning

Deti

April 22, 2000

While we lived at the Gran Canaria Hotel, Gita and I waited on tables and brought in a little money. But now that we had moved, that income was gone. It was time for us to find another job. Before we got deported, that was the least we could do to help Mom and Dad.

It was a warm day, the sky a deep blue and clear, without even a wisp of a cloud. Perfect for job hunting. We put on some of Mom's makeup, and Gita suggested wearing the high-heel trainers Dad had bought us in Albania—anything to make us look older, at least older than fourteen.

She and I set out early in the morning for the Folkestone town center, where a number of restaurants and hotels were located. Gita did the talking for the two of us, and soon we had made the rounds at several places. Most of the managers gave us a quick answer. No. Either they didn't have any openings or they recognized immediately that we were too young.

Finally we were down to one possibility: the Blanc Hotel restaurant. The boss, Mr. Martin, a stocky, balding man with piercing blue eyes, still hadn't said yes or no.

As he studied us, my stomach tightened. Maybe like the others, he was already thinking we were too young.

"So you're both interested in a job?"

"Yes, we are." We straightened our shoulders to stand taller.

"Well, we do have an opening. How old are you?"

"Sixteen," I said.

"And we have experience," Gita added. "We worked at the Gran Canaria Hotel for five months."

Mr. Martin smiled. Maybe he didn't trust us, or maybe our baby faces betrayed our age.

"Bear with me a minute until I speak to the manager," he said.

I grabbed Gita's arm. We had a chance. *Please, God, please make this happen!*

Mr. Martin returned with a plump woman about Mom's age. "I'm Claire." She extended a hand to each of us. "So you've both waited tables before?"

We nodded, and Gita launched into her speech about our job at Gran Canaria. We were hard workers, she said. They wouldn't regret hiring us.

"Well, as Mr. Martin told you, we have an opening." Claire paused. "When would you be able to start?"

"Tomorrow?" I said without hesitation.

"Sounds good."

Was this real? A new job! And it was all because of Gita. I would have done anything for her right then, including giving her my Del Piero T-shirt.

"One thing, though," Claire said. "I'd like only one of you to start tomorrow, and the other twin next week. Simply because you are so identical, it will be very confusing for us all." She laughed and Mr. Martin joined in. "Then once you learn the ropes, you can work together."

"That's perfect," Gita said.

She was about to explode with excitement, just like me, but we had to compose ourselves and look professional.

"So what are your names?" Mr. Martin asked.

How silly of Gita—she memorized the whole speech and forgot to introduce us with our fancy names. Before leaving the house that morning, we had talked about changing our names so no one would know where we worked. If the school kids found out, they might give us a lot of trouble.

I answered first. "I'm Alexa." I now had the same name as Alex Del Piero.

Claire pointed to Gita. "And you are?"

Smiling, Gita didn't answer right away. Uh-oh. Not good. She always hesitated when she wasn't sure what to say. That shouldn't have been a hard question. I stepped on her foot. *Come on, last night you said you wanted to be called Sara.*

She swallowed. "My name is Gita."

I coughed hard to let her know she had just ruined our plans. Maybe she could tell them her middle name was Gita? English people had more than one name.

Claire offered me a glass of water. The poor woman had no idea that my sister was the cause.

Gita said nothing, continuing to smile, while Mr. Martin and Claire cheerfully chattered on. Like so many people, they asked if we had any distinguishing marks to make it easy to tell us apart. I tried hard to be in their game, but I was furious at Gita.

The hotel mostly catered to elderly people, Claire said, and all we had to do was take orders, serve meals, and clear the tables afterward. She would train us, and we would work three or four shifts a week. Each shift lasted three hours, and Mr. Martin would pay us £3 an hour, which I learned was the national minimum wage. In Albania, people would get that amount for a full day's work.

If Gita and I each worked twelve hours a week, together we could save £312 a month and help Dad pay off the debt. And maybe if we were really good at our jobs, in the future we might work twenty hours a week. That would be £520 a month. Then perhaps we could also send some money to Grandma Lako and Grandma Lira and buy them presents for Christmas.

❧

During the first two months of work, our skills quickly improved. The elderly hotel guests boosted our confidence and brightened our day after all the horrible hours at school. No one had figured out yet that we were twins.

One night, a customer in a bright yellow shirt sitting at table three waved me over. I had just served the starters a few minutes ago. What could he want? I approached him with a friendly smile. "How can I help you, sir?"

"I'm very impressed by you, young lady. Can you please tell me your secret?"

"Sure, if I know it myself."

Laughing, he pointed to table twenty-three on the other side of the restaurant. "How did you go from that table over there to the other side of the restaurant in three seconds? I have to say, in all my sixty years, I've never seen a waitress as fast as you. Gosh, where do you get all that energy?"

Of course, he was confusing me with Gita. "Thank you, sir. Please tell my boss so he'll give me a raise." I gave him a cheeky smile.

Three nights later, I persuaded Gita to play along with me when we waited on new customers. There was only one problem: Nikki, the supervisor, a young pregnant woman, barely twenty, with wild green eyes and long, messy brown hair. Her deep voice and determined expression made her seem much older. She scared me. She had already yelled at me twice when she had mistaken me for Gita and expected me to serve her tables.

To pull off our little joke, Nikki needed to stay away from us. But even if she did find out what we were up to, Gita wouldn't be in trouble. I would get all the blame.

"Go ahead," I told Gita. "If Nikki sees you now, you're not doing anything wrong. You're just serving your tables."

Away Gita went to table six to meet the new customers. From a distance, I watched her write their orders on her pad. She laughed and joked with them, appearing to have a good time.

I finished serving my table. By the time I placed the order in the kitchen, I calculated that Gita would have left table six. I had to play this part well: come across as polite and confident while being prepared to control my laughter. When I arrived at table six, the two elderly couples stopped talking and looked up at me.

"Hi, dear, is everything okay?" one of the women asked.

"Yes, madam, and good evening. How are you all doing?"

"We're doing fine," said the bald-headed man seated next to the woman who had just spoken.

"That's good to hear." All four pairs of eyes were locked on me, surely everyone wondering why I was there. "Well . . . ," I said slowly, "have you decided yet?"

"What about, dear?" the bald-headed man asked.

"About what you would like to eat, sir?"

The two women laughed.

The bald-headed man peered sharply at me. "Darling, are you okay?"

"Never been better."

"But you took our starter orders two minutes ago. We ordered four tomato soups. Don't you remember?"

"Oh, you're right. I did take your order. Four tomato soups. I confused the table number. I'm terribly sorry."

"Don't worry, young lady," the bald-head man said.

Back I went to tell Gita that the first step was done. Soon after, she brought the four soups to their table. Once they had finished, I took the empty bowls to the kitchen, and then Gita returned to tell everyone that their main order would be out shortly. When Gita disappeared from view, I approached the table and said the same thing.

The bald-headed man frowned and eyed me carefully. "Darling, are you *sure* you're okay?"

"I'm fantastic!"

"Well, I hope so, because you were here not a minute ago and told us the same thing."

My mouth opened in feigned surprise. "Oh, I'm so sorry, everyone. I'm really embarrassed. This is my second mistake. Can you please accept my apologies? I must be having problems with my memory."

"Of course, dear," the bald-headed man said. "As long as you don't forget to bring our order."

"I can assure you, I won't forget." I smiled sweetly at each of them and left the table as quickly as possible to keep them from asking any more questions and guessing what was going on.

Gita served the main course, and soon it was time for dessert. After seeing her take their orders, I went to table six again, hoping that I wasn't playing with fire. I paused, pretending to think hard. "I took your desert orders, didn't I?"

"Yes, you did," all four guests said at once.

"It was four bread and butter puddings. Remember?" the bald-headed man said.

"Oh, yes, sure."

They didn't suspect a thing. I had played my role well.

I met Gita in the kitchen, and we planned our next move. It was time to end our game. Now we would both go out together. I picked up two bowls of pudding, and Gita picked up the other two. We approached table six in single file, walking closely to each other, our footsteps in rhythm. The eyes of all the other diners were on us. Finally we arrived. One of the women took off her glasses as if she couldn't believe what she was seeing. Then she wiped her glasses and put them back on. "Oh my God, I'm seeing double. There are two of you!"

The other woman laughed. "You look so identical."

"So did you both serve us?" the bald-headed man asked. He pointed at Gita. "Was it you who took our food orders for the second time?"

I raised my hand and grinned. "No, it was me, sir. You mixed us up."

"It looks more like you mixed us up!" The man laughed heartily, and the others joined in.

The diners watching us also laughed. Now everyone knew about the "double trouble twins" of the Blanc Hotel.

CHAPTER 25

Surprises

Gita

June 2, 2000

Deti, Mom, and I stared at the white envelope in Dad's hand bearing the Home Office insignia in the left-hand corner. I couldn't help but think it was bad news. Dad slit open the envelope, unfolded the letter, and handed it to me to translate and read aloud. I grimaced, the anticipated disappointment already forming a tight knot in my stomach.

Long ago, I had lost hope that we would be allowed to stay in England. So many Albanians had been sent back. Now it would be our turn.

I raced over the neat paragraphs of print. Nothing made sense. I rubbed my eyes and took my time to absorb each word, each sentence. I still didn't understand.

Again I went back to the beginning, reading even more slowly. Did this letter really mean what I thought it did?

"Come on, Gita!" Dad said. "What does it say?"

"I was wrong." I looked at each of them, blinking away the tears.

"Wrong about what?" Mom said. "What do you mean?"

"I was wrong about being pessimistic!" I shouted, waving the letter excitedly. "We won! We won!"

"Gita! Tell us what we won," Mom said sharply.

"We get to stay in England for two more years! Our IND is to be extended until July 2002!"

Like all the air rushing out of a balloon, the fear and tension vanished from the faces of my exuberant sister, mother, and father. It was such a magical moment—I wanted it go on forever. We hugged and kissed, holding onto each other, feeling such joy and excitement, such utter happiness.

I had forgotten what happiness really felt like. It would take a while to digest the news, especially since I had already convinced myself to expect the worst.

For the rest of the day, we celebrated with chocolates and soda, Mom and Dad with white wine. Home Office had also sent a letter to Ikie, our lawyer in London, informing him of our extended stay. Two more years! Thank God Dad no longer had to spend sleepless nights by the window watching for police cars—and finally Deti and I could focus on school and work.

In two years, many things could change. If Deti and I continued to work, we could possibly save enough money to repay our entire debt. The future seemed bright. Now all we had to deal with was the present.

June 7, 2000

We had grown accustomed to the bullying from our classmates. During the entire time we were at school, we had to have eyes in the back of our heads. Every chance they got, they picked on us.

Even though waiting on tables at the Blanc was tiring work, it was a welcome change from school. The customers were always kind and friendly to us. Still, I couldn't help feeling trapped in such a monotonous routine. At four-thirty every afternoon, Deti and I arrived home from school, and after a thirty-minute break, we dressed for work in our white shirts and black skirts.

It took us a half hour to walk to the hotel. The paid working hours started at six o'clock, and we usually left for home between nine and nine-thirty. Sometimes it was later, depending on whether the customers were on time for their reservations.

I was ashamed to admit that I'd become so angry about my life that I didn't think I could keep it all to myself anymore. I wanted to shout out loud about how miserable it was in England. I wanted to complain about all the things that were wrong. I never had to work in Albania—why did I have to work now? Where was the fun? The joy? The entertainment and the games? Why couldn't I just be a kid for a few more years?

With the anger came guilt. Mom and Dad surely didn't deserve my complaints. They had sacrificed so much for us two, how dare I complain about working?

Claire at the restaurant knew we needed the money. Whenever anyone called in sick, even if it was at the last minute, she'd phone us at our home and ask us to come in. Deti and I always said yes. How could we pass up the money? Yet I resented it when Claire called, especially when I was looking forward to flopping down on the sofa and mindlessly watching TV as soon as I came home from school. But I had no choice. I was only a refugee who would probably leave England in a couple of years. I needed to help my parents.

At least Deti and I could work together. At the end of the shift, we shared all the customer tips. I could endure the pain in my legs and feet from running back and forth in the restaurant and the exhaustion afterward if I knew I would get at least two pounds in tips.

Normally we clocked in at 5:40, but that particular Wednesday we were late because it took me so long to fix my hair. It was frizzy and stringy, and I couldn't get it to stay in a neat ponytail. I even tried wetting it down and doing lots of comb-throughs, but it still didn't fall into place. The harder I tried, the messier it looked. I gave up before Deti could shout at me that we would be late. My hair would simply have to do.

We ran all the way to the hotel. When we arrived, I went straight upstairs to the restaurant so Nikki could see we were on time.

Soon after, I felt a pull on my arm. "Gita," Deti said, "you need to go downstairs and clock in before six. Hurry!"

How could I have forgotten? I whirled around and made a leap for the staircase. At the end of the week, Claire would check my clock-in time, and I didn't want to be recorded late.

As I approached the bottom steps, I heard someone talking. "I can't wait to get my first paycheck." The voice was sharp and hard.

A second voice answered, but it was too muffled to make out.

I leaned forward to see who was there, hoping the second voice wasn't Claire, because then she'd know for sure I was late. At the bottom of the stairs, I saw the backs of two short, skinny girls, a blond and brunette. The blond inserted the cardboard pad inside the metal time clock.

Who was she? By now, all the girls working that night would have checked in. I scrambled down the last couple of steps. I recognized their voices but couldn't place them. Where had I heard them before?

The blond girl turned sideways, still talking to the brunette. I was close enough now to see her face. Small blue eyes as familiar as her voice. I had looked into those cruel eyes many times at school. They mocked and taunted me, wounding my heart. They were one of the reasons I hated school so much.

And now I knew who the brunette was. I'd been on the receiving end of her cutting remarks far too often.

Neither of the girls saw me. I slowly turned around on the steps and headed upstairs, fear welling up inside me. How the hell could they be here? It was impossible.

A month before, Mr. Fox nearly suspended both of them for accosting Deti and me as we walked into the school assembly building. The girls had commanded us to get down on our knees in front of them, and when we refused, they started swearing at us and throwing stones. Mr. Fox gave them a final warning. But he couldn't do anything here.

My head was spinning. My shock turned into anger and disgust, sucking all the energy from every limb of my body. As if it weren't enough that these witches made my life hell at school, did they have to show up at work and make my life miserable here too? How could this be happening? It was all so ugly, so . . .

Maybe it was my imagination. Maybe it wasn't them after all. No, I was sure it was them—skinny, short, and evil. *Evil.* Yes, that was what they were. One thing I knew for sure. If those two were working here, I'd quit. Forget about clocking in. Where was Deti? I had to find her and tell her the terrible news.

I spotted her putting bread and butter on the side plates. Grabbing her elbow, I led her to the corner of the restaurant where no one could see us. I didn't have to say anything. She read the anxiety on my face. "What's wrong? Is it Nikki? Did she tell you off?"

I shook my head. "Much worse." My voice choked up.

"What?" she asked, panicked.

"I—I—they—the—those . . . Deti!" I chattered on so fast she couldn't understand a word.

She moved closer. "Calm down, Gita! What is it?"

"They—those beasts from school—you know who I mean."

"Which ones? There are so many!"

"The ones who asked us to kneel down, the ones Mr. Fox—"

"Yes, so? What about them? Why are you even mentioning them?"

I tried to get a hold of myself and talk slower. "Listen to me, please. They're here. At the Blanc Hotel. I just saw them. Our school enemies, those two who torment us at school are our new coworkers!"

"*What?*" Deti stared at me. The large bread basket she was carrying fell from her hands and dropped onto the carpet. All the color drained from her face. "You must be kidding. Those two vile, foulmouthed witches? Those vampires? Are you sure?"

"Yes, yes, I'm sure. They were by the time clock when I went down to—they were . . . they were . . ." I started to tear up.

"Gita! Come on, tell me this is a joke."

I shook my head.

"Please tell me this isn't true," she whispered.

"It's true. I'm not kidding. It's our worst nightmare." I wiped my eyes with the back of my hand.

"If they work here, we leave."

"That's exactly what I was thinking, and—"

"Alex and Gita!" Nikki interrupted us. She stood just inside the kitchen door, calling to us in her most officious managerial voice.

The hell with Nikki. The hell with everything. As Deti and I marched toward her, my heart beat faster. She would probably introduce us to the witches. So what should I do? Shake hands with them? I didn't even have a chance to discuss it with Deti. Right then, I wasn't afraid of Nikki. I was too angry and upset to be afraid.

I stepped ahead of Deti, straightening my shoulders, playing the role of waitress about to go on duty who was conferring with her manager. I would pretend everything was okay. Yes, everything was okay—though my stomach was in such turmoil I couldn't imagine how that would ever be possible.

As I approached the kitchen door, I saw the two girls standing by the stove. "Yes, Nikki. What would you like us to do?" I focused on Nikki, watching the two of them out of the corner of my eye.

The blond frowned and turned toward the brunette, giving her a tap on the shoulder as if trying to wake her up from a bad dream. Her face was contorted. Clearly she was angry, wondering how this could be happening to them. How could they end up working at the same hotel as these two refugees? These *outlanders*?

Deti stood still behind me. I would be brave and look at the girls directly. Their expression was dull, indifferent. They weren't afraid of us. They despised us. I turned back to Nikki.

"So, Gita and Alex . . ." Nikki paused.

"Yes," Deti said faintly.

"These two lovely young ladies are starting here tonight."

The blood rushed to my head. I was so revolted I was going to be sick. *Lovely ladies?* Nikki would never be on our side. We could never tell her the truth about them.

Deti and I said nothing. I had been a good actress so far, but how could I pretend that the past didn't exist? How could I pretend that we would work well with two girls who had caused us so much suffering? How could I forgive them without their asking for forgiveness?

At the same time, I hoped and prayed they wouldn't remember that my twin sister's name was actually Detina and not Alex. I couldn't even think what would happen if they did. We would be in such big deep trouble, and it would be our own fault. Because we lied to the hotel management about Deti's real name, we would be the bad guys, and these two witches would tell everyone at school about it. Even Mr. Fox wouldn't trust us anymore.

What should we do? If we quit, then at least we wouldn't have to deal with this awful situation. And we wouldn't have to see their nasty faces almost every day. We would never have a good working relationship with them. This was only the beginning—the worst was still to come.

But wait. Why should we have to be the ones who quit? We started working here before they did. If we quit, they would be so happy about it. I couldn't give them another trophy. We came here first. I wasn't a poor, stupid, useless girl. Not only was I a good student, but I was also a good waitress, and the customers really liked me. I had to fight for what I deserved.

Standing in front of them, I wouldn't give them the satisfaction of sensing my discomfort, and I certainly wouldn't speak first.

"Hi, nice to meet you. I'm Daisy," the blond said.

"I'm Caroline," the brunette said after an awkward silence. Both girls were on edge now. Maybe they were getting the message.

Deti and I said a quick hi in monotone unison, without saying our names.

"Gita," Nikki said sharply, "today you're going to work with Caroline." Nikki didn't detect anything. She was all business, the way it should be. "Since it's her first shift, I expect you to explain to her what we do. Please make sure you both work as a part of a team. You have twenty-five customers between yourselves. That shouldn't be difficult."

"Sure," I said as casually as possible. She had no idea what she was putting me through. Grimly I offered her a tight smile.

Deti was assigned to work with Daisy. I was more concerned about Deti than I was about myself. Daisy was a worse monster than Caroline. If Daisy tried to provoke Deti and pick a fight with her, the whole restaurant would become a war zone. It would be so embarrassing for both of us. And then Daisy would tell everyone about it at school. A perfect reason for all the kids to gang up on us again.

Caroline followed me into the kitchen. My thoughts raced as I automatically picked up the knife, sliced the rest of the bread, and placed it in the basket so I could finish Deti's task.

"What do you want me to do?" Caroline asked, giving me a fake smile.

"You can put the butter on the side plates," I said in a flat tone.

Obediently Caroline picked up the butter crock and entered the dining room after me. I spotted Deti arranging the silverware on the tables. Her head was down. Daisy wasn't with her, and Nikki had just left for Sainsbury's to buy some orange juice. I slipped over to her. "Are you okay?"

"I'm as okay as you are," she said softly.

"Look at me, Deti." She lifted her eyes to my face. "I thought about it and came to the conclusion that we don't need to worry. They can't do anything to us here. *They* have to depend on *us* while we train them. There's no reason why we should quit work. We have to be strong. Think of them as just silly kids."

I was quaking inside. *Very good, Gita. Very brave. A great act. Nothing to worry about—ha!* Who was I kidding? I wouldn't say anything to provoke a fight, but I also knew how evil the two girls could be.

At least for the time being, I had managed to reassure Deti. A few minutes later, I had another chance to catch up with her alone in the kitchen, but before I could say anything, Caroline and Daisy approached us. They smiled at each other and then looked at us like they wanted to say something. Deti took a couple of steps forward until she was standing in front of me, preparing to fight if necessary.

I counted their steps as they drew closer. One, two, three—boldly, directly. My throat tightened. Now they were only a step away, their expressions smug and self-confident. I shuddered inwardly.

"Hey, twins," Daisy said, "do you need some help?"

"Not at the moment," Deti said coolly. "But thank you."

Caroline turned to me. "You'll let me know what to do, won't you?"

"Yes." Short, abrupt.

"It is a bit awkward, isn't it?" Caroline said softly.

My heart was pounding. I tried to keep a poker face, but it was very hard to hide my emotions.

"Can we just forget about the past and make a new start?" Daisy asked.

Did I hear her correctly? My cheeks got hot as her words echoed in my head. *Forget about the past? Make a new start?* One part of me was relieved, and the other part of me was seething with anger. How could they be so calm? As if they hadn't done anything at all to us? Just forgive and forget?

"We already have," Deti's voice cut through my anger. It rang with confidence. Deti! I was so proud of her. I was afraid she was going to say something she would later regret. She had taken over and also saved my feelings.

Deti removed a stack of tea cups and saucers from the kitchen shelf and gave half to Daisy, who was smiling. I would like to think it was an apologetic smile. They went out to the restaurant and placed four tea cups and saucers on each table.

I collected the menus, struggling to forget the past. It had no place here in the present, I reminded myself. I swallowed my anger as Caroline followed me into the restaurant and asked to take half the menus.

We worked together, side by side. Caroline asked questions about work. She smiled constantly, perhaps to reassure me that she wouldn't hurt me anymore, that she was now a nice person.

But I didn't trust either one of them.

CHAPTER 26

Nothing Is Greater Than Love

Deti

June 15, 2002

Almost three years had passed since we first arrived in Folkestone. By then, it felt like we'd been there forever. I sorely missed Albania, but the thought of going back to visit our grandparents, Frida, and Lela, seemed like a distant dream.

The bullying persisted, though by now Gita and I had developed thicker skins. The kids finally found out where we lived, and they came at night and bombarded our windows with stones. Luckily, they hadn't broken any of them yet.

I was mostly worried about Dad. A week before, when the boys hit our windows for the fifth time, he was so furious he took me with him to the house where one of the bullies lived to tell his parents about the vandalism.

Just as I could have predicted, it was an exercise in futility. Who was my dad after all? A foreigner. A man who spoke broken English, who had to use his daughter as a translator. I could read the hatred in these people's eyes. I could read their minds. *Get out, you foreigner. You don't belong here! That's what our son is trying to tell you. Don't you understand?*

It hurt me deeply to see Dad treated this way. I could see how heartbroken he was. On the way home, I tried to change the subject, all the while thinking that never before had I ever physically felt the pain of fear, especially in my chest, around my heart. I was afraid Dad might feel worthless because he was unable to protect us. Of course, it wasn't true—but did he believe it?

Gita and I told him again and again that his love was our sword and his word was our shield. But that wasn't good enough if Dad didn't believe it too. How did these ignorant, bigoted adults who let their kids get away with bullying and reckless vandalism compare to a man like Dad? A man who was good through and through and who would have severely punished his children for such cruel, destructive behavior toward others?

There really was no comparison. So what had made me lose faith in him? What had made me afraid that these people could hurt him? He was bigger than all of them! What did the Golden Rule say? Would he ever have treated anyone the way we were being treated?

At once I brightened up. I squeezed Dad's hand, and he gave me a loving squeeze in return. He might be disappointed, but he wasn't defeated.

Gita and I still waitressed at the Blanc Hotel, picking up a morning shift as well. Over the past year, Mom and Dad had gotten jobs there too.

Because our parents still struggled with English and our immigration status was so uncertain, it was difficult for them to find work. Soon after Gita and I had begun at the restaurant, we asked Mr. Martin to consider hiring Dad, and he did. People really liked Dad—he was friendly, worked hard, and never complained about anything. Starting out as a dishwasher, he would eventually be promoted to assistant chef. In Albania, he'd had a prestigious job, but like many refugees, he couldn't translate that into something similar in England.

Mom started at the restaurant one year after Dad, helping in the kitchen. Mr. Martin owned a small fish and chips place, and it wasn't long before he moved her there. No one could cook fish and chips better than Mom.

⚜

As time had gone by, Gita and I greatly improved our English language skills. At work nobody doubted that my name was Alex, and at school, I avoided Caroline and Daisy, just in case they called me Alex instead of Deti.

The biggest surprise to us both: Caroline and Daisy had become our good friends. The other day I walked home with Caroline and she even bought me a burger with chips. Whenever I thought about their first day working at the hotel and how furious we were—so angry and disgusted, we wanted to quit—it made me laugh. So many things could change in a year. I learned to never, ever judge a book by its cover.

Now Caroline respected me, and I respected her. We accepted one another for who we were, despite sometimes having different thoughts and different ways of doing things. You don't always have to agree with someone to be a good friend. On Sunday Caroline asked me to go with her to buy some fags. I didn't know what the word "fag" meant, and assuming it was a kind of candy, I said yes. She mentioned something about my being sixteen years old so I wouldn't have any problems getting them. Why would you have to be sixteen to buy candy?

Then she explained that cigarettes weren't sold to anyone under age sixteen. Caroline was only fifteen.

I refused to go. Caroline called me a boring woman who lived by the Golden Rule and we both laughed. Now that I knew her, I felt sorry for her. She didn't have it easy. Her mother was an alcoholic, and her dad, a drug addict, had left them two years before. Caroline always had a smile on her face. I surely never would have known anything sad was going on in her life if she hadn't told me.

Two years ago, I thought Caroline was the lucky one, that she had everything, and Gita and I were the only ones with problems. Our family didn't have our citizenship papers, we were in debt, and at school, we were treated as outcasts.

Now I saw us as the lucky ones. We had a loving, caring family. Our parents sacrificed everything for the two of us. Caroline was paying the consequences of her parents' mistakes. That made me sad. I reflected on this for a long time and realized that maybe that was why

Caroline was aggressive at school. She was suffering, very hungry for love, so she lashed out at others for being unfair to her. She had a little brother named Harry she loved dearly. When Harry was in trouble, he called Caroline. She didn't let anyone hurt him. Harry looked up to Caroline for everything. We were not very different after all.

I would miss not seeing Caroline at work. We had asked Claire for four weeks' leave so we could study for our GCSE exams coming up soon—General Certificate of Secondary Education. We would have to do well in all the subjects to get into a good secondary school.

But we'd have to study for nearly the entire summer and not have a single chance to enjoy it. I could already see the early morning sun sparkling on the rooftops and lighting up the clear blue sky. I could smell the salty ocean air and feel the warm sand scrunching between my bare toes. None of that would be mine this summer. Instead, I would be cooped up in the house with textbooks and notepads, cramming my brain with possible test questions and answers. Day after day—as life went on so freely and beautifully outside. It wasn't fair.

And besides that, the World Cup was underway, and Gita was being a huge pest about it. Not until she was convinced that I was fully prepared for the exams would she stop trying to keep me from watching my soccer hero Del Piero play striker for Italy against the other European teams.

Still, GCSEs were important to us. Gita took them so seriously that her worry about doing well took priority over the bullying at school. She didn't get offended as easily anymore. She probably figured it was a waste of her good energy to let them bother her. Time was tight. We had to focus on the exams.

On the calendar posted on the wall of our bedroom, Monday, June 17, was highlighted with a red pen. Over the date, Gita had written, "9:15 a.m./Main school building/English exam."

Only two days away. I was a bundle of nerves, and sometimes it was hard to concentrate.

John Steinbeck's novel *Of Mice and Men* was one of the books we would be tested on. Thank God this morning our good friend and brilliant English student Sophia was on her way over to study with us.

We cleared off the large green chair in preparation for her arrival. That was Sophia's chair. The seating arrangement was intentional, so Gita and I could sit on either side of her. "A rose should always sit between two thorns," Sophia said. This made us laugh, for in this case, she was our English rose.

She gave us confidence, and both Gita and I were hoping to get an A—at least in English literature because we had a deep heart connection with this novel by Steinbeck. Possibly it was because Gita and I felt a close kinship with George and Lennie.

In the book, George says to Lennie, "With us it ain't like that. We got a future. We got somebody to talk to that gives a damn about us."

Lennie responds, "Because...because I got you to look after me, and you got me to look after you, and that's why."

CHAPTER 27

Missing in Action

Gita

June 25, 2002

It was a quarter after nine in the evening, well past the time Mom and Dad said they'd be back. On Deti's lap, the GCSE science review book was open to the same page as it was an hour ago. She kept looking over at the clock, making me nervous, like she did in Albania while waiting for Dad to come home from work. Then and now, I found it impossible not to get caught up in her fears.

Deti glanced over at me apologetically, almost sorrowfully, because she knew her negative moods annoyed me. I started to say something but stopped. Seeing so much fear in her eyes, I couldn't lecture her. When we were young, those eyes were innocent. Too soon, her eyes, like my own, recorded terror and pain far beyond our years.

Mom and Dad had left for their walk a couple of hours before, and though rain was predicted, it was mostly clear then. The sky was striped with beautiful pinks and roses as the sun lowered toward the horizon. Another magical summer evening by the harbor.

It was nearly dark now. Mom and Dad were probably having such a lovely stroll by the seaside that they had lost track of time.

But still.

Out the window, a gust of wind lifted the branches of the trees and swept an empty cardboard box down the lit street. It tumbled over and over.

Maybe it wasn't Deti after all, but me. Maybe she was reflecting my anxiety. Had I ever stopped living in fear that something bad might happen? No. I had to be honest with myself—I was still afraid. The past still breathed inside me, inside both of us. It still lurked in the shadows of every thought.

I checked the clock again. Nine-thirty. Right then, I was as worried as Deti about Mom and Dad. It was late, even if they had decided to linger a bit longer than usual.

Three more minutes ticked by. I couldn't stand it anymore. Casting aside my review book, I jumped up. "Deti, c'mon. We've done enough studying for the exam. If we don't know the material now, we'll never know it. Let's go find Mom and Dad and walk home with them."

Deti closed her book and looked up at me with relief. "Thank you!"

Throwing on our jackets, we locked the front door and walked toward the harbor. The weather forecast was right after all. The temperature had dropped, and the air felt heavy with moisture. I could smell the approaching rain. We ran along Earls Avenue toward the beach, the wind at our backs. It tossed our hair in our faces, pushing us forward.

At the high walls of the red brick church, we slowed down to catch our breath. The church always had a calming effect on us. In the early morning before we went to work, when everything was dark and quiet outside and the stars still shone overhead, we loved to run like crazy, racing each other until we reached the church.

Then we would laugh and dance in the middle of the street, shouting, "Jesus, we love you!" Our voices bounced off the tall gray buildings next to the church and echoed back to us, "Jesus, we love you!" During those times, we were two happy, free spirits.

Not tonight. We couldn't linger. I made the sign of the cross and prayed for Mom and Dad, and we took off running again. We reached the harbor shore, my cheeks burning, the sweat cooling my neck. Finally, in the middle of path that followed the road leading to the beach, I spotted Mom and Dad trudging up the small hill.

Deti saw them too. "There!" She pointed to the two of them. "Thank God they're okay." She bent over and rested her hands on her knees, breathing heavily as if to get rid of all her pent-up anxiety.

Mom and Dad were walking arm in arm, looking strong together and so much a couple. I inhaled deeply and filled my lungs with the moist ocean air, letting myself enjoy the peace and serenity that swept over me.

Mom saw us and waved. Hand in hand, Deti and I ran toward them, never taking our eyes off this beautiful picture of them. But as we draw closer, the image vanished. Something wasn't right. I studied them more carefully. Dad was leaning heavily on Mom. I felt a strange quickening in my gut, a foreboding.

When we reached them, Mom asked, "What are you doing here? Did you finish reviewing for the science exam?" No hello, no smile. Her face was tight with worry.

"Yes, we're done," I said, glancing at Dad. His shoulders sagged with exhaustion.

Deti frowned. She noticed too. "Dad, are you okay?"

"Yes, I'm fine," he said slowly, as though he were having trouble speaking.

Deti and I moved to either side of him and each took a hand. He shuffled forward, stopping every so often to take a breath, leaning on our shoulders to keep his balance.

"What is it? Please tell me," I said.

"It's just a headache. Nothing to worry about."

"But, Dad, you can barely walk," Deti said gently. "We need to go to the hospital."

"No, I'll be okay. You should be thinking about your exams tomorrow."

The twenty-minute walk to the house was the longest of my life. Inside, Dad said he was going to take a shower, and he and Mom climbed the stairs to the bedrooms. I could only hope he would feel better soon.

Deti and I sat on the living room sofa, both of us needing to do something to take our minds off Dad. I picked up the remote and switched to Channel 4 where the movie *My Father, the Hero* was about to start. In no time, we were absorbed in the adventure of a divorced dad who takes his fourteen-year-old daughter Nicole on a tropical vacation to the Bahamas.

Suddenly, strange sounds came from upstairs. I looked at the clock. Not even ten minutes had passed. "Deti, turn down the volume. Did you hear that?"

"No, I–"

"Come quick, girls!"

We bolted up the stairs, taking them two at a time. Dad was lying on the carpet in front of the bathroom door covered with a white towel, his hands on his chest, his mouth clamped shut. His eyes were out of focus, and he didn't respond when I spoke to him.

Mom was crumpled in a heap by his side. "He's dying!" she screamed hysterically.

I glared at her. "Never say that, do you hear me? Dad will be fine!"

Deti burst into tears.

I hated both of them. Just when I needed them most, they were falling apart. I couldn't let their fear get to me. "Deti, get the coffee and raki."

"Run!" Mom screamed.

Deti raced down the stairs.

I turned to Mom. She was rocking back and forth, weeping uncontrollably. "When did he lose consciousness?"

"About two, three, minutes ago, while he was taking his shower."

Seconds later, an ashen-faced Deti handed me the white coffee tin. Trembling, I lifted the lid, pinched out some coffee grains, and inserted them inside Dad's nostrils. Mom wet his lips with some raki. No change. His eyes were still blank.

"Dad, wake up. Please wake up."

I raised his chin so he could breathe. Still no response. "Dad, do you hear me?"

Miraculously he moved his hand. His eyelids fluttered slightly, and then he looked up at me. "I'm cold," he whispered. "My chest hurts."

I covered him with a blanket while Mom took his temperature: 104. "Dad, stay strong. We're calling the ambulance. You'll be all right."

I squeezed his hand and flew down to the kitchen, Deti right behind me. I picked up the phone, but my mind went blank. What was the number?

Neither of us knew. We had never called an ambulance before.

Darting out of the house, we went to the neighbors' and pounded on the door. The woman living there never spoke to us. Her daughter was one of the bullies at school, but now we didn't care. Nothing mattered except getting help for Dad.

When the woman opened the door, I blurted out, "We need an ambulance. What's the number?"

"Uh ... 999," she said, her eyes wide with surprise.

"Thank you!" we both shouted over our shoulders.

Back inside, we ran to the phone. I dialed 999, my hand shaking, and then put it on speaker.

A man answered. "Emergency. Which service do you require: fire, police, or ambulance?"

"Ambulance!" we said together.

A woman came on this time. "Your phone number and the address of your emergency?"

I told her, talking over Mom's loud sobs from upstairs.

The woman launched into a series of questions, and we took turns answering them quickly. "Our dad collapsed ... he's forty-five ... yes, he's breathing ... 104 ... no alcohol ... he doesn't smoke."

"Chest pains?"

"Yes," Deti said. "He might be having a heart attack."

"Is he conscious now?"

I rushed to the stairs. "Mom, is Dad awake?"

"Yes ..." She let out a shuddery breath. "But he has a terrible headache. And he's so cold."

I rushed back to tell the woman.

"When will the ambulance get here?" Deti asked.

"Within twenty minutes."

"Please hurry!" Deti said. "We're so scared for him."

"Do you want me to stay with you on the phone until it arrives?" the woman asked.

I looked at Deti, and she shook her head.

"No," I said to the woman, "but thank you."

After we hung up, Deti said, "We should call Mrs. Bytyci."

"Good idea." I searched for her number in Mom's contact notebook on the counter. She was Mom's Kosovar friend who lived nearby with her husband and their three kids close to our age.

I found her listing on the second page and dialed, again putting the phone on speaker. When I got their answering machine, I spoke softly so Mom couldn't hear. "Mrs. Bytyci, please come over as soon as you can. Dad is very ill. We're going to the hospital."

"We need your help," Deti added, her voice breaking.

Mom might be upset with us for making the call. She never wanted to be a nuisance, but this was an emergency.

I ran upstairs. Dad was shivering badly even though Mom had covered him with two more thick blankets and had turned him on his side. It hurt to see him like that.

"Dad, how do you feel?"

"I'm cold," he said feebly.

"The ambulance is coming." I lifted his hand to my lips and kissed his clammy skin.

"Where's Deti?" he asked.

"She's downstairs. I'll get her."

Deti was pacing in the living room. Tears streamed down her face, a balled-up tissue in her hand.

"Come upstairs. Dad is asking for you. If he finds out you're down here crying, he'll worry and that will make him worse."

She looked at me uncertainly for a moment and then went to the bathroom to run a cloth over her eyes before heading upstairs. I followed behind. Her steps were reluctant and slow. I could feel the deep pain tugging at her heart.

Dad was still lying on the carpeted floor. Shakily Deti bent down, touched his hand, and smiled.

"Have you been crying?" Dad labored over each word.

"Of course not, Dad. There's nothing to cry about. You'll be fine." After taking a long, hard look, she straighted up and quietly tiptoed down the stairs.

When I heard the outside door open and close, I dashed to the window. Was that Deti leaving? Yes, there she was. It was now raining heavily. I could barely make out her form. She was running away from the house, head down, fleeing from anything bad that could happen.

Why did she do these things? *Oh Deti, I don't need this.* I returned to Dad and pretended that nothing was wrong.

He was sleepy. I talked nonstop to keep him awake, all the while staring at my watch—as if that could make the hands move faster.

I could hear the ambulance siren in the distance. I ran downstairs and flung open the front door. As I waited for the three paramedics to reach the house, two men and a woman, I searched the wet street for Deti—no sign of her.

Upstairs, the older male paramedic stooped over Dad. "Mr. Zalli, can you hear me?"

No response.

The younger man knelt down and felt Dad's pulse. "His breathing rate is low and so is his pulse. His temperature reads 103.6." He gave Dad an injection.

"Gita, what is he saying?" Mom asked anxiously.

"He said that Dad will be fine." With the paramedics now taking charge, I could relax a little. They knew what to do.

"Mr. Zalli, can you hear me?" the young man kept asking.

Dad managed to nod this time.

"Mr. Zalli, we aren't sure what's going on, but it's very important for you to come to the hospital with us so the doctors can examine you and prescribe the correct treatment. We have to go now. Are you okay with that?"

I translated for Dad, and again he nodded.

After transferring him to a gurney, they carried him downstairs and wheeled him into the ambulance. Dad slowly moved his head from side to side, his eyes searching for something.

"Ready to go, guys?" the ambulance driver called out.

"Where is Deti? Why can't I see her anywhere?" Dad asked, pushing out each word with difficulty. "Where is Deti?"

How was I going to tell him that she had run away? I needed to invent a clever answer.

"Dad, we have to go." I tried to keep my voice calm, but inside I was panicking. "Deti has gone to the store to buy some aspirin."

"I'm not going unless I see her," he said.

"What is he saying?" the woman asked.

"He isn't willing to go to the hospital until he sees my twin sister."

"Where is she?"

"I don't . . . I don't know."

It was now just past eleven-thirty. I felt so alone. I looked up at the sky. *Don't do this to me, God. Please bring her back, bring her back now.*

Ten minutes passed and still no sign of Deti. The ambulance wasn't moving. Dad didn't want to go without her.

Even Mom was becoming suspicious. "Where is this store?"

Before Dad could ask me more questions about Deti, I told him that she probably wasn't back yet because she had to go to the store that stayed open late.

How long would I have to keep lying to him? What if she didn't come back?

All I wanted was a trace of her, the tiniest indication that she was on her way home. I gazed down the street, and through the heavy mist from the pouring rain, I saw a slight movement. Was I seeing things? I strained my eyes to check again. Yes, someone was approaching!

Actually, two people, and they were walking along Earls Avenue.

One of them was a girl, but I could hardly make out her shape. It was so dark and foggy. Was it Deti? But who could be with her? When she left the house, she was alone.

My gut told me that the girl was my sister. A tall young boy was walking next to her. Their shapes became clearer now. It *was* Deti—but who was the boy?

I raced down the street and hugged her. She was soaking wet. "Deti, where the hell have you been? We're going to the hospital! And don't you think I'll just forget about this! We'll talk about what you did tonight when Dad is better."

"Will . . . will he make it?"

"Yes. He's in safe hands. Now let's go quickly. And tell Dad that you went to get some aspirin for him."

Later I learned that when Deti ran out the front door, she went to "our" church, where she sat outside in the rain, crying and praying for Dad. A boy who happened to be walking down Earls Avenue heard her loud crying, and when he found her sitting there in the rain, he insisted on taking her home.

I climbed into the ambulance next to Mom. The IV attached to Dad's arm and the oxygen mask on his mouth reflected the gravity of the situation. The two male paramedics monitored his heart with an electrocardiogram.

"Dad, I brought the aspirin," Deti called weakly into the back of the ambulance.

Dad struggled to lift his head to see her. "Come on in."

I nodded to her, but she shook her head.

"Actually, there's no more room in here," I said. "Why don't you sit with the driver?" That way, Dad wouldn't see how upset she was.

"Yes, come up front with us," the driver said. "Hurry, we should go."

After we took off, my eyes met Mom's. She had finally stopped crying.

I stroked Dad's arms and talked to him all the way to the hospital. "The doctors will help you," I said, acting as if I knew this to be true.

So much uncertainty—and so much I wanted to say but couldn't.

The iron bars around my heart kept me locked and frozen. But one thing was for sure. I would never give up. Never.

Ahead of us, the road was clear of traffic as the driver sped up. In the front seat, the paramedic sitting next to Deti asked her to open her eyes and remove her hands from her ears. "Everything is going to be all right," she said.

Deti refused to listen. She was escaping reality.

I couldn't do that. I couldn't hide. One of us had to be strong, and Deti gave me no choice.

CHAPTER 28

A Real-Life Test

Gita

June 25, 2002

The driver did his best to get us to the hospital as quickly as possible, but it still took twenty minutes. At last the Harvey Hospital ER entrance appeared in front of us. Deti opened her eyes and unblocked her ears. Five doctors came running as the three paramedics transferred Dad onto a long white gurney. An older doctor wearing a white coat and stethoscope started talking to him.

"Can you hear me, Mr. Zalli?"

Dad didn't respond. The doctor repeated the question in a louder voice, "Mr. Zalli, can you hear me?"

Again, no answer.

The doctors ran down the hallway, pushing the gurney as fast as they can. "Emergency room!" they shouted.

I could hardly breathe. My dad was immortal, or at least he was until a few hours ago. Was it actually possible that we would lose him? What would I do without him? How would we live? No. It couldn't happen. We needed him.

He was such a good person. *God, please save him.*

A pale Deti clung to me. "Gita, let me go to the waiting room. I can't see Dad like this. And I don't want to hear any news."

"Okay, stay there." I pressed her hand reassuringly and followed the doctors into the emergency room.

They were all talking at once as they injected Dad with a colorless liquid. He wasn't regaining consciousness, and Mom was out of control again. "Doctor, do something! He can't die! Please save him!" She tugged at a paramedic. Gently he placed an arm around her and ushered her out of the emergency room.

Now it was only me with Dad and the doctors. I clutched the cross around my neck.

"How long has he been feeling like this?" the doctor in charge asked.

"Just today. He had a headache," I managed in a small voice that must have been mine.

"He's responding slowly. His heart rate is going up."

I tightened my grip on the cross. *Please, Dad. Please wake up.* A few minutes later, he opened his eyes.

"He's okay." The doctor in charge squeezed my shoulder and smiled.

Relief washed over me. In the waiting room, Mom was curled up in a wooden chair, talking to herself and wiping her tears with her white handkerchief. It was as if she had surrendered and was already grieving. Deti was kneeling on the floor, eyes closed, ears blocked with her thumbs. She moved her head from side to side as she prayed.

Many other people were sitting in the room, waiting for their own news. A thick cloud of uncertainty and dread hovered over them. With sorrowful eyes, they gazed at Deti's kneeling form, sensing her fear and pitying her as they were pitying themselves.

I hurried over to her. As she turned to me, she shook her head, her face wet with tears. Forcefully I removed her thumbs from her ears.

"Stop behaving like a coward. Dad is alive. He woke up. He's going to make it."

She jumped up and threw her arms around me. Pulling back, she asked, "But what if he doesn't live? What will happen to us? How will I live without him?"

"Don't be so pessimistic. God will help Dad. Trust me."

"Is Dad awake?" Mom hovered over us, her voice shaky and tearful. I nodded.

"Thank you, God." She sighed deeply and hugged both of us tightly. I realized how much I needed her comfort and protection.

"Let's go to Dad," I whispered.

Holding hands, we went down the hall to the emergency room. From the window, we could see Dad lying in the white hospital bed, surrounded by four doctors. His eyes were closed. Did something happen again?

The doctor in charge noticed us and gave us a thumbs-up. Dad must be sleeping, or maybe the doctors put him to sleep. Behind closed doors, we couldn't hear anything, but we could watch the four doctors discussing Dad's case. An interminable ten minutes passed until the doctors emerged from the room.

"How is he? What's the diagnosis?" I asked the doctor in charge.

He smiled at the three of us. "He's better. We need to run more tests before we know anything else."

"Can we see him?"

"Not just yet. Give him about thirty minutes."

Thirty minutes! How could we possibly wait that long? The round white clock in Dad's hospital room read 1:45. It had been such a long night. I tried closing my eyes, counting seconds. I opened my eyes again, checking my accuracy against the second hand on the clock. But now both hands were standing still, refusing to move forward. They were frozen, like me. It felt like nothing was moving anymore. I looked away and then looked back again.

It was two o'clock. Fifteen miraculous minutes had passed.

I closed my eyes. I thought about all the times when we were younger, when Deti and I were having so much fun playing with our friends and we hoped the time would never pass. Or when we were in school taking an exam and we wanted plenty of time to answer every question correctly, to check and recheck.

And now here we were, trying to force the hands of that clock to move ahead another fifteen minutes as fast as possible.

Almost forty-five minutes after the doctors had left the room, one of them reappeared in the waiting room. "Your dad is okay now. You

can go see him. We have transferred him to another room." He led
us down the hall.

We opened the door carefully in case Dad was asleep. His small
white room was full of machines that seemed more alive than he was,
each beeping and humming with its own set of sounds and rhythms.
They were connected to him with all sorts of tubes and wires, as
though he were surrounded by a swarm of snakes.

A large tube extended from his open mouth, and a pool of yellow
liquid sat in its curve. Taped on his chest were several wires hooked
to a machine on the left of his bed that traced the heart rhythms, appearing as patterns on a screen. Next to this machine was a blood
pressure monitor.

All the equipment was scary. I'd seen pictures of it in my biology
textbook, but never up close, connected to a live person. The message these machines were delivering was one I didn't want to hear:
Dad's condition was critical. I reminded myself that the tubes were
doing everything they could to stabilize his condition. Yet he looked
so powerless, his face drawn and his skin so pasty it almost looked
like a mask. All I wanted to do was cry, but I wouldn't let myself.

Two nurses brought chairs into the room, and one handed Mom
some black coffee. We moved the chairs next to the bed so we could
stay close to Dad. I held his hand and Deti's. She never stopped
praying.

At some point, I must have fallen sleep. When I opened my eyes, it
was morning and the clock read eight. In front of me was a short,
thin woman wearing black slacks and a white shirt. I rubbed my eyes
to make sure it wasn't a dream. No, the woman was really here, right
by my side.

"Mrs. Bytyci!" Deti said.

Mom and her dear friend hugged each other tightly. "How did you
know?" Mom asked her.

"The girls called me last night and told me about Gimi, but I only heard the message on my answering machine this morning," she said. "I'm so terribly sorry. How is he doing? What do the doctors say?"

"We don't know yet," Mom said softly, holding back her tears. "The doctors didn't give us any specific diagnosis. They're going to check on him again this morning."

"I pray to God he'll recover soon."

With Mrs. Bytyci at the hospital, I felt safer. Mom was finally sharing her worries with another woman, someone a lot older than Deti and me, whose judgment she could trust more than ours. Mrs. Bytyci's warm words filled our hearts with hope—the only precious thing we had left.

Dad's eyes fluttered open. The sound of our voices had awakened him. He looked different, more alert. He smiled weakly at all of us.

Mrs. Bytyci greeted him, and Dad was able to ask how she and her family were. Deti and I kissed him gently on the forehead.

"You're . . . still here?" he asked.

"Of course! Where else would we be? We'd never leave you alone."

"I know . . . but . . . don't you have a science exam today?" Dad was having difficulty speaking, and his voice sounded flat and tired—but he remembered our exam.

Deti's mouth opened wide with astonishment. I knew what was going through her mind. Instead of thinking of his own health, his own critical condition, Dad was thinking about us.

"Ah, yes, the science exam," we both said at the same time. "We forgot about it."

"But shouldn't you go? It's very important."

"Only if you're okay."

"I'm fine." He nodded slightly.

Until yesterday, my biggest fear had been getting a low grade on an exam or not showing up to take it, especially this one. Since Deti and I both wanted to become doctors, today's exam was the most critical of all the secondary certification exams. But that didn't scare me anymore. I didn't even panic. Perhaps I had just passed one of our real-life tests.

Yes, we needed to go. Even though we knew we would risk not getting an A, we couldn't run away. Dad would never want us to do that. He taught us to be fighters, to face any situation. No matter how difficult the challenge, we had learned to confront it head on without trying to hide or make excuses. Today we would take the exam and do our best.

"You're tired, but I know you'll do well," Dad said.

"Sure, we'll do well," Deti said. "We'll do it for you."

"I'll take you to school," Mrs. Bytyci said. "The exam is at ten." She looked at her watch. "We'd better leave now if we want to get there on time. Let's go, girls!"

Deti and I kissed Dad's hand, gave Mom a hug, and followed Mrs. Bytyci to her car. I looked down at my slacks and shirt. How could we go to school? We weren't wearing our uniforms. But we didn't have time to go home and change. Mrs Bytyci said we'd be getting into morning rush-hour traffic, so it would probably take us about fifty minutes to get to school. If we were lucky we would get there by ten, exactly when the exam began.

Mrs. Bytyci was an expert driver, weaving us in and out of traffic. This was the first time I'd been with an Albanian woman driving a car. Somehow she managed to get us to school just after nine-thirty.

Outside the main hall, where the science exam was about to take place, we still had a few minutes before we needed to go in. Several of the students had already arrived. Most of them had their science books open, doing a last-minute review. Unlike us, they looked nervous.

For the first time in our lives, we didn't review thirty minutes before the exam. Usually we kept our books and notes open as long as we could.

Sophia caught sight of us. "Deti, Gita, where have you been? Where are your uniforms? Why aren't you reviewing? This isn't like you."

Neither one of us could get the words out.

"What's wrong? You can tell me."

"We've been at the hospital all night," I managed to tell her, my voice trembling. "Our dad lost consciousness."

"Oh! Is he . . . is he okay?"

"He's a little better," Deti said.

"What can I do to—"

The school bell cut into Sophia's sentence. Her "Good luck!" floated over the tumult of students entering the room.

At a quarter of ten, Mrs. Brown started to give instructions. "You have two hours to answer all the questions. Please use a black pen. If you finish early, raise your hand and I will come get you."

Deti was sitting in front of me. She turned slightly to look at me and blow me a kiss, her eyes shiny with tears. "Good luck!" she whispered.

Why did she do that to me? Why did she always know how to hit my weak spot, just at the wrong time? I had held back my tears for over twelve hours, the entire time we were at the hospital, and now I felt powerless against all the pent-up fear and anxiety. The first dry sob escaped from my throat. I looked down at the two wet splotches on my exam paper, followed by two more.

Deti was also crying, and like me, she couldn't stop. All I could hear were Dad's words: "You will be fine. I love you." This made me cry harder.

Mrs. Brown noticed that something was wrong and came over to our desks. Within seconds, everyone was looking at us. She asked a few questions, and we told her about our all-night experience at the hospital. Getting us each a glass of water, she reassured us that Dad would recover. "Are you going to be able to take the exam?" she asked us anxiously.

We nodded. Yes, we would do it, especially for Dad. By that time, our exam papers were soaked through. Mrs. Brown gave us fresh copies, and we wiped our tears. It was time to forget the pain, be strong and concentrate on doing our best on the exam. For Dad. Totally for Dad.

After we passed in our papers, Deti and I didn't discuss the answers the way we usually did. Instead, we ran outside to meet Mrs. Bytyci, who was waiting for us.

"Come home with me and spend the rest of the day and night with us," she said.

Deti and I shook our heads politely. "Thank you, but we'll be all right," I told her.

"Then I will come over to your place and sleep there tonight," she said firmly. "The kids will be fine with their dad. Here's my cell phone. Call your mom and let her know that I'll drive you back to the hospital after we get some lunch."

We both thanked her.

She laughed. "Now that's more like it. You girls are so pretty when you smile."

We told Mom that the exam went well and that we would see her and Dad soon. Mom didn't understand anything the doctors said about Dad's current condition other than the word "okay."

When Deti and I arrived at the hospital, the doctors told us they still hadn't come up with a diagnosis. They thought Dad might have had a stroke. But the worst was over, they said. He was safe now.

A week later, he was discharged from the hospital, and Mr. and Mrs. Bytyci brought him home. We shall always be eternally grateful to our dear friends.

To our surprise and delight, in spite of our exhaustion, in spite of the fear and uncertainty of Dad's recovery that weighed heavily on our minds when we entered the building that day to take the GCSE science test, both Deti and I received two of the highest scores in the school.

Deti and I also got the highest scores in all the other GCSE exams as well. And we were awarded the silver cup for two consecutive years for our fluency in French and Italian. Despite all the bullying, despite holding down a job during most of the time we were attending the Channel School, we had triumphed.

CHAPTER 29

The Hope of Morning

Gita

September 2004

When our beloved dad lost consciousness and had to be rushed to the hospital, our perspective changed. Though he was only in his mid-forties, we learned that he had suffered both a heart attack and a stroke. Confronting death can be a sobering experience, and our close call with Dad had made us much more aware of the things that really mattered.

Nothing, positively nothing, was more important than good health. And stress was one of the most debilitating ways to ruin it. By default, over the past decade, my father—all of us—had collected more than the ordinary amount of stress. We had paid a heavy toll for our harrowing experience emigrating from Albania to England, followed by not months but years of uncertainty. Even though the Home Office had extended our stay for yet another two years, we lived in constant fear of that fateful knock on the door, never knowing if we would be deported.

Added to this anxiety for Dad were the burden of the loan that had to be repaid, his inability to earn a good living in a country whose language and customs were foreign, and constant worry about his family's safety and comfort.

Yet with the bad often comes the good. Deti and I proved that even under duress we could stay focused and strong. Our excellent GCSE scores in science and every other subject allowed us to study at the Folkestone Grammar School for Girls, the best secondary school in town.

That isn't to say that our past experiences at the Channel School hadn't left their marks. During our childhood years, certainly neither of us had suffered from rejection from our peers or from low self-esteem. Every day we looked forward to school and spending time with our friends afterward.

In England, all of our self-confidence had been stripped from us. Refugees, especially those from the so-called Slavic countries, were considered outsiders. We fell to the lowest rung of the social ladder.

Nevertheless, we managed to prevail. Even though we might not have been able to lead a normal teenage life in England, at least we had continued to excel in school. Like any warriors, after a few assaults from our enemies, we developed a set of survival skills that served us well.

Since Italians were perceived higher than Albanians on the immigration scale, we told everyone at the Folkestone Grammar School that we were from Italy. As if by magic, our classmates started liking us and all the name-calling and bullying vanished.

Over time, we developed strong friendships with three girls in our class. Though they probably wouldn't have cared that we were Albanians, we still kept a safe distance. Whenever they asked us to come to their homes, we used work as an excuse because at some point, we would have to return the invitation. These girls were wealthy. What would they have thought of our humble home in comparison to theirs? Would they still be our friends? We didn't want to take any chances. Instead, we went out with them during free periods, and now that we had pocket money, we enjoyed a coffee or a pizza.

We started becoming more independent too. We no longer had to wear uniforms at school. It was fun to be able to shop for clothes, and for the first time, Deti and I dressed differently from each other.

In addition to learning how to be grateful for our family's health and for a sense of belonging somewhere at last, during those two years since Dad was rushed to the hospital, we continued to mature physically, emotionally, and spiritually. We were always together, always side by side.

We managed to repay our $12,000 loan—a huge weight off our shoulders. With more money to spend on food, we could eat a healthier diet.

Pursuing careers in medicine meant we had to study hard to get qualifying grades. Our efforts were rewarded when both Deti and I received straight As on the entry tests.

Yet excellent grades weren't enough for us to be accepted at one of the medical schools. Permanent residency in the UK was a basic requirement. Otherwise, we would be classified as "overseas students," requiring us to pay the annual college tuition of £11,500 each.

Deti and I persisted. After several more phone calls and letters, the dean of admissions at the University of Sussex gave us a conditional acceptance. We needed to provide proof of indefinite leave to remain in the UK within two weeks of the beginning of the classes.

At once we contacted Jenny, our social worker. Every other week, our family visited her to receive cash assistance and to discuss any issues that we wanted to bring to her attention. We helped with her Albanian cases by serving as translators for refugees who couldn't speak or understand English, so she had become a good friend.

Jenny knew how much our immigration status meant to us, so she contacted our lawyer and Home Office on our behalf. She reported to us that Home Office had approved new laws, making our family eligible for amnesty. That meant we would be able to earn indefinite leave to remain in England.

But our struggle still wasn't over. Home Office had no specific procedure in place yet for addressing each case. It could take many months before we received amnesty status. Together with Jenny, Deti and I called Home Office many times and left messages, explaining our current situation.

Just in the nick of time, our hard efforts paid off. Home Office came through, and our family was granted indefinite leave to remain. We no longer had to fear that we would be sent back to Albania.

There are no words to describe our immense relief.

Soon after, both Deti and I received scholarships in the molecular medicine program at the University of Sussex.

At eighteen years old, we were only on the cusp of understanding what life was all about. We surely didn't know everything about ourselves. Past experiences had defined who we were then, and the future would be determined by the steps we took from that point forward. Those steps would depend on our intentions and our goals. Did we really know what we wanted? Were we willing to work hard? That was the blueprint for success that our parents and school teachers had taught us. Know what you want and then go for it. Accept all challenges. Never run away or hide.

Although eighteen years is a relatively short time when compared to a normal life span, our tumultuous uprooting and the many ensuing vicissitudes had already matured us well beyond our age. Our journey had been filled with hardship, suffering, and disappointment, but we had stopped considering those obstacles as our enemies. Instead, we now saw them as growth opportunities.

Mom said that scars fade with time. Perhaps one day the scars of fear still locked in our hearts would disappear. When we could finally release those fears, we would emerge stronger and more resolved than ever to align ourselves with happiness, hope, and success. But if those scars didn't fade altogether, whatever remained would serve as a badge of achievement, reminding us of how far we had come and how much we had accomplished.

Our homeland would always be Albania, a beautiful country in southeastern Europe, where we learned how to walk, speak, play, love, and respect others. Those were the qualities we brought with us to our new life. They served as the backbone for a future rich with promise.

We weren't afraid of the unknown because we discovered that maturity had everything to do with the acceptance of uncertainty.

We learned from the past as we lived in the present and created the future. As long as the sun set in the evening and rose the next day at dawn, as the artists of our destinies, we knew that together as twins yet separately as individuals, each of us would paint the hope of morning.

Epilogue

Deti

Our lifelong dream to become doctors was within our grasp. But our course changed the first time we used a microscope to study cells. A whole new world opened up for us. Soon after, we both decided that scientific research was the direction we wanted to take.

I loved learning new things every day, excited by all the experiments we ran. Being a doctor was important, but it was more of a routine job. Gita and I were eager to make breakthrough discoveries in medicine.

In 2012, I received my PhD and graduated from the University of Leicester in biochemistry, and Gita received her PhD and graduated from the University of Birmingham in immunology.

I applied to Harvard School of Dental Medicine for postdoctoral research and was accepted into the program. Although I didn't want to be separated from Gita (the first time ever), she encouraged me to accept the offer and moved to Boston to be with me for the first month.

While at Harvard, I conducted high-impact research in the field of cell biology, and in collaboration with world-recognized scientists, I published in an important scientific journal. For this, I received the Young Investigation Award in Science, and for two consecutive years, I was awarded the dean's scholarship for best scientific research.

I also lectured and organized multiple courses for both undergraduate and graduate students in the fields of genetics, biochemistry, and cell biology with world-class professors and Nobel Prize laureates. At the age of twenty-four, I was one of the youngest lecturers and course directors.

Inspired by former US president Barack Obama, I actively participated in the Harvard professional government, organizing multiple conferences, including the Harvard Leadership Conference and the Harvard Lectures That Last event. I was a member of the Education Committee at the American Society of Cell Biology (one of America's larger cell biology conferences), in addition to directing the Harvard Biotech Journal Club for all research scientists and healthcare professionals.

After six years at Harvard, I returned to England, where I worked as a senior academic at the University of Oxford in oncology. I am currently working at the University of Cambridge as the director of Pre-Medical Studies. Fascinated with science in space, I had the honor of graduating in early 2023 from NASA's Spaceflight Technology, Applications, and Research Program, which focuses on the principles of conducting spaceflight biological experiments.

Beyond my wildest expectations, I was nominated one of the top one hundred successful Albanians in both the United States and England.

Gita

My postdoctoral work was at University College London. I conducted medical research in the fields of immunology and psychobiology, collaborating with world-leading scientists, including a Nobel Prize winner, and published highly acclaimed papers in research journals.

While at University College, I discovered a passion for teaching. I taught postgraduate medical students, along with directing neuroimmunology courses, for which I was awarded the medical students' top teaching award. I also served as a tutor and supervisor for students in the biomedical sciences master's program.

From there, I moved on to Imperial College London, where I conducted medical research in the field of hematology and continued my teaching career, designing, developing, and directing biomedical science courses in one of the most innovative and prestigious university programs in the world. In 2020, I earned a master's degree in university teaching and learning.

Being passionate about teaching and learning in higher education, I have focused over the past few years on promoting teaching excellence. Currently, I am working as a learning design lead for Imperial College, directing the design, development, and delivery of fully digital and blended learning projects for the faculty of medicine as well as for undergraduates in medical bioscience. I collaborate closely with academic colleagues to create excellent, pedagogically sound learning experiences for students.

I have also been awarded senior fellowship of the Higher Education Academy, in conjunction with the Supporting Teaching Accreditation and Recognition Framework. As part of the review panel, I help promote teaching excellence by recognizing professional academics who are dedicated to enhancing their teaching skills in higher education through ongoing professional development.

The love Deti and I share for science and medicine led us to launch We Speak Science, a nonprofit organization whose aim is to enhance science education worldwide. To achieve our goals, We Speak Science has gathered a global team of medical doctors, scientists, pharmacists, and medical students who review and translate the latest medical research articles into participating countries' native languages. Through the We Speak Science international network, medical professionals worldwide are able to access and utilize this information for their own research and clinical practice.

Deti also founded the Zalli Foundation (I am the cofounder), a nonprofit that educates, elevates, and inspires people globally through the art of storytelling while promoting empathy, kindness, and positive mental health. In collaboration with We Speak Science and the world's most prestigious universities, Deti and I have helped more than 20,000 students globally.

Over the last few years, we have been invited to appear on several TV programs in Albania, Macedonia, and Kosovo, where we discuss the goals of our foundations as a vehicle for augmenting science and medical education in the developing Balkan countries.

Our family returned to Albania for the first time in December 2005, six years after we left. By that time, Deti and I were eighteen and in college, no longer skinny kids. Of course, all our cousins had changed too.

Mom was able to see her mother again. Grandma Lako lived another eight years, passing away in 2013. Grandma Lira and Grandpa Llazi are still alive. At age ninety, Grandpa is fit and smart, but Grandma, two years younger, has Alzheimer's disease—she forgets often. They still live in Bubullimë, and Dad talks to them twice a week.

Our dear friend Lefta moved to England, and she and Axhem got married. They have three children. We discovered that Axhem really is a prince.

Deti and I both have families of our own. I married Redin in 2012, and we have two boys, Amos and Ambrose. In 2015, Deti married Tony, and they also have two boys, Destin and Soleil. We live close to our parents, and all of us get together as often as possible.

Acknowledgments

The completion of this book would not have been possible without the assistance and support of so many people whose contributions are sincerely appreciated and gratefully acknowledged. While it is not possible to enumerate everyone, we would like to express our deep appreciation and indebtedness particularly to the following people: Fadil Berisha, Lefta Cela, Axhem Cela, Simon Morley, Anna Whittaker, Mark Kosmo, Christian Botting, Gentiana Pambuku, Nevila Selmani, Oliver Goodyear, Sallyanna Curd, and Victoria Robinson.

To the Voice of America Journalists for Albania, who promoted our story and our book, especially Arben Xhixho and Menada Zaimi; and to Harvard University, for organizing an event dedicated to us and our story.

To J. D. Freedman and Paul Jensen, who encouraged us and supported us with the book.

To Sandra Jonas and her team at Sandra Jonas Publishing, for believing in us and bringing our story to fruition.

To our mother and father, the heroine and hero of our lives. Both of you inspire us every moment by being extraordinary parents, grandparents, and friends.

To our grandparents, aunts and uncles, and friends, who believed in our dream and made our journey to England possible. We are so grateful to you all.

To our husbands, Redin and Tony, for your endless support, encouragement, and kind understanding throughout the writing process.

And finally, to our sons: Amos and Ambrose, and Destin and Soleil, who light up our lives every day. We hope that by reading this book, you will learn more about your origins and feel proud of your roots.

Photo Album

Top: the twins' parents, Dita (*left*) and Gimi Zalli, c. 1982;
bottom: Deti (*left*) and Gita, about three months old, 1986.

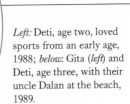

Right: Deti (*left*) and Gita, age three, 1989.

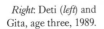

Left: Deti, age two, loved sports from an early age, 1988; *below*: Gita (*left*) and Deti, age three, with their uncle Dalan at the beach, 1989.

Left: Gita *(left)* and
Deti, age five, with
their dad, 1991.

Right: Gita *(left)* and Deti,
age six, on their first day
of school, 1992; *below:*
Deti *(left)* and Gita *(right)*,
age twelve, with a friend
a year before they left for
England, 1998.

Above: Gita (*left*) and Deti with their mom on their nineteenth birthday, 2005; *right*: Gita (*left*) and Deti, age nineteen, on a pedestrian bridge in London, 2005; *below*: Gita (*left*) and Deti, age nineteen, with Deti's hero Sylvester Stallone at the Madame Tussaud wax museum in London, 2005.

Top: Deti (*left*) and Gita, age nineteen, with their mom, 2005; *bottom*: Deti (*left*) and Gita, age nineteen, sightseeing with their parents in London, 2005.

Gita (*left*) and Deti, age thirteen, on the Folkestone Beach in Kent, England, 1999.

About the Authors

Born in Albania, twin sisters Argita and Detina Zalli were eleven years old when the government collapsed and anarchy broke out. Two years later, after several failed attempts to flee the violence and poverty, they escaped with their parents to England.

Overcoming the formidable challenges of being refugees, both young women achieved academic success and went on to become highly accomplished PhD research scientists and lecturers.

Influenced by Barack Obama and eager to help others, they founded We Speak Science, a nonprofit organization that supports disadvantaged students throughout the world, particularly immigrants, whose circumstances hinder their ability to learn at school.

Subsequently, in collaboration with world-class oncologists and scientists, Argita and Detina cofounded Afërdita Ime, a nonprofit initiative that seeks to help cancer patients through psychosocial support and counseling.

Argita and Detina live with their husbands and children in London.

Made in the USA
Middletown, DE
20 January 2024

48232495R00151